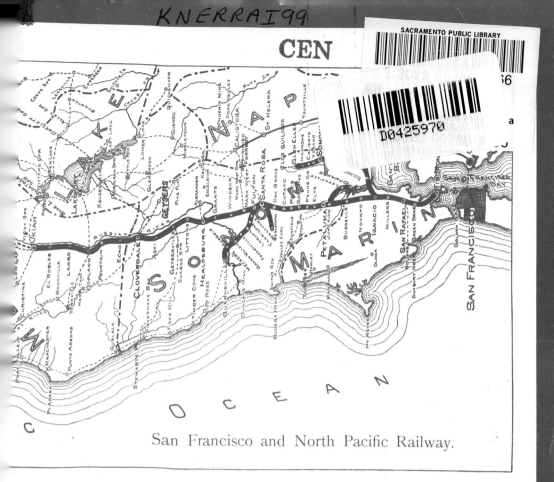

San Francisco and North Pacific Railway.

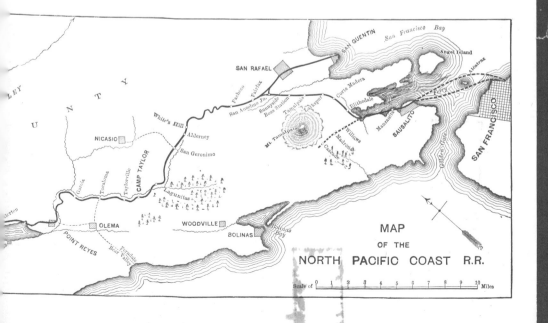

MAP
OF THE
NORTH PACIFIC COAST R.R.

Scale of 0 1 2 3 4 5 6 7 8 9 10 Miles

REDWOOD RAILWAYS

A STORY OF
REDWOODS, PICNICS AND COMMUTERS

by GILBERT H. KNEISS

1956
HOWELL-NORTH
Berkeley, California

Published by the Howell-North Press
Printed and bound in the United States of America by the publisher.

Redwood Railways

SCENE FROM NORTH PACIFIC COAST RAILROAD
from an old Danish magazine of unknown date

FOR EMILY AGAIN

Foreword

As THE universally recognized *doyen* of railroading writers in the field of the Old West, Gilbert Kneiss is singularly well equipped to explore the little railroads and their country ways that first brought the light iron of their primeval operations to Northern California and then grew up into the Northwestern Pacific.

To be sure some of the carriers he chronicles here had rich connections or relatives, but their operations were none-the-less characterized by the pastoral simplicity, at least in their earliest years, that was to endure into the Twentieth Century only in the short lines of the land long after the main roads had acquired chairmen of the board and were occupying twenty or thirty pages in *The Official Guide*.

There was a peculiar charm and intimacy about the homespun operations of the first railroads in the West. Often they were of country origin, their comings and goings those of suburbia removed at its farthest possible extreme from cities and the ways of cities, their rights of way grassgrown to the point of actual impediment of progress, their locomotives of the genus teakettle.

To encounter an actual facsimile of what railroading even on the most important lines must have been in the age of the iron dawn-horse, one must go today to the most obscure, remote and improbable short lines in the Deep South, railroads forgotten by time and, mercifully, unknown to what passes for "progress". The author of this brief foreword remembers, and that within the decade, helping to "wood up" an ancient wood burner on the Mississippi & Alabama near Vinegar Bend, a railroad whose general manager had only recently heard of Appomattox.

He remembers, too, the enchanting simplicity of its drinking facilities of the Amador Central when, only a few years ago, it ran in steam from Ione to Martell, a wonder and glory of the California countryside. The water storage facilities of the teapot mounted on not precisely round wheels that passed for its only motive power were not sufficient for the twelve miles of the trip to Martell, and a stop was made in a meadow half way between nowhere and nowhere. Here the entire train crew of four descended and wrestled manfully with a contraption of gutters, sluices and flumes which led precariously from a hillside reservoir to the tender, one span of which depended on being suspended from the shoulders of the fireboy. At least a third of the water got to the engine as it waited patiently in a meadow and after a pause that refreshed everybody but the member of the crew who held up the center span of the aquaduct, the train went bravely on.

It is of railroads that started thus, aye and in even more primeval fashion, that Mr. Kneiss has written in this knowledgeable monograph. On one of them, the eagle eye even doubled as tallowpot to work both sides of the cab alternately, and on more than one, smoke orders were unknown, since there was no other train to constitute opposing traffic on the entire railroad, one engine being sufficient for one railroad. Others were proud local roads with a stable of carefully burnished woodburning 4-4-0's. Yet they all became important pawns in the wider transportation rivalries carried on by the Big Four and other frock-coated, well-heeled nabobs.

This is the theme of Mr. Kneiss' excursion into the redwoods of Marin County and its adjacent marches in the golden noontide of California the Golden. For his gentle landfaring into history, the faithful, who travel in steam forever, doubling the hill and widening the throttle on the tangents, are in Mr. Kneiss' debt.

LUCIUS BEEBE

VIRGINIA CITY
1956

Acknowledgements

It has been my good fortune in the preparation of this book to have the assistance of some of the actual participants in the incidents related and of the descendants of others.

Among these are the late Eugene de Sabla, Mr. Paul Foster, Judge Edgar Zook (son of chief engineer Zook of the San Francisco & North Pacific Railway) and Mrs. Du Val Moore, the daughter of John Martin. Others equally helpful include Mr. E. Denman McNear of Petaluma, Mr. Robert H. Menzies of San Rafael, the late J. W. Mailliard, Jr., Albert Dutton (the nephew of Warren Dutton and one of the first employees of the narrow-gauge), Mr. L. V. Korbel, and Mr. H. S. Graham, assistant to the general manager, Petaluma & Santa Rosa Railway.

Miss Florence Donnelly of the Marin County Historical Society was very helpful and Mssrs. Gerald M. Best and Fred A. Stindt are, in large part, responsible for the locomotive rosters in the Appendix.

My appreciation is also extended to the Bancroft Library of the University of California and to the Public Libraries of Petaluma, Santa Rosa, San Rafael and Ukiah, as well as to the Society of California Pioneers for invaluable assistance. Specific reference material is listed in the Appendix.

For their kindness in loaning photographs I am grateful to Mssrs. Jack Farley, Roy D. Graves, Donald W. Howe, Ken Kidder, Addison Laflin, Arthur L. Lloyd, Jr., the late Stanley F. Merritt, Wallace Sorrel, Louis Stein, Lloyd Stine, E. W. Tompkins, J. E. Turner and William Waste.

My appreciation also to Erle Heath and Richard Houghton of the Southern Pacific Company who kindly read over the script in galley proof.

All possible effort has been made to avoid mistakes, but in many cases the records are thin or almost non-existent. So it is likely that in spite of everything some errors have crept in and it is hoped that these will not mar too much what, I believe, is a true picture of early day railroading in the Redwood Empire.

GILBERT H. KNEISS

BERKELEY, CALIFORNIA
1956

Table of Contents

Chapter		Page
I.	THE COWS AND CHICKENS LINE	1
II.	THE BATTLE OF THE PAPER RAILROADS	7
III.	THE BOY WONDER	13
IV.	THE COMMUTER IS BORN	21
V.	PETER DONAHUE AND THE CAL. P.	27
VI.	BRIEF INTERLUDE WITH THE BIG FOUR	37
VII.	THE NARROW GAUGE GETS STARTED	41
VIII.	A RAILROAD FOR THE GOPHERS	55
IX.	THE LEAP FROG LINE	65
X.	LUXURY ON A SLIM TRACK	71
XI.	COMMUTER HANDICAP	79
XII.	THE KING IS DEAD!	85
XIII.	IRON HORSES AT HUMBOLDT BAY	91
XIV.	THE RAILS REACH UKIAH	97
XV.	PICNICS WERE NO PICNIC!	101

Chapter		Page
XVI.	THE PRINCE DIES TOO	105
XVII.	NARROW GAUGE JINX	111
XVIII.	JOHN MARTIN TAKES OVER	118
XIX.	"JUICE" LINE CHALLENGE	125
XX.	GIANTS BATTLE TO A DRAW	130

Appendices

List of locomotives 139

Excerpts from an annual report 147

References 159

Index 163

List of Illustrations

Page

Early scene from North Pacific Coast Railroad . . . . frontispiece

Asbury Harpending at age of 16 12

Green Street Wharf, San Francisco, 1869 . . . . *facing* 14

San Quentin Landing in the '60s . . . . *facing* 15

Train approaching San Rafael . . . . *facing* 15

Locomotive BULLY BOY . . . . *facing* 30

Locomotive SAN JOSE . . . . *facing* 30

San Anselmo in 1875 . . . . *facing* 31

Locomotive OLEMA . . . . *facing* 31

Locomotive M.S. LATHAM in trouble . . . . *facing* 46

Train on White's Hill . . . . *facing* 46

Mill Valley in 1889 . . . . *facing* 47

Locomotive VALLEY FORD . . . . *facing* 47

Elim Grove in 1886 . . . . *facing* 62

Locomotive VALLEY FORD in San Rafael . . . . . . *facing* 62

Sausalito terminal of the North Pacific Coast . . . . . . *following* 62

Locomotive SAN RAFAEL . . . . *following* 62

Mill Valley Station in 1898 . . . . *following* 62

Locomotive BULLY BOY (N.P.C. No. 8) . . . . . . *facing* 63

S.F. & N.P. advertisement 63

Running Gear and "Prism" 66

Norfolk Terminal of the S. V. Prismoidal Ry. 67

North Pacific Coast folder 69

San Rafael "Union Depot" in the '90s . . . . *facing* 78

San Rafael Salt Water Baths in the '80s . . . . *facing* 78

Locomotive PETALUMA . . . . *following* 78

Page

Train leaving Hopland in 1893 . . . . *following* 78

Locomotive SANTA ROSA . . . . *following* 78

Locomotive "COFFEE GRINDER" . . . . *following* 78

Point Tiburon . . . . *following* 78

Ferry *San Rafael* . . . . *following* 78

Ferry *Tiburon* . . . . *following* 78

North Pacific Coast train in the redwoods . . . . *facing* 79

Train leaving Tiburon in the '90s . . . . *facing* 79

Steamer *City of Lakeport* advertisement 89

Eel River & Eureka No. 1 at Eureka . . . . *facing* 94

Eel River & Eureka ferry *Oneatta* . . . . *facing* 94

Eel River & Eureka No. 1 EEL RIVER . . . . *following* 94

Depot at Fortuna . . . . *following* 94

Van Duzan River trestle . . . . *following* 94

Humboldt & Mad River Railroad . . . . *following* 94

Humboldt Logging Railway at Freshwater . . . . *facing* 95

Advertisement of house raffle 95

Milton Latham's private car MILLWOOD . . . . . . *facing* 126

E. H. Shoemaker, John Martin, R. R. Colgate and Eugene de Sabla *facing* 126

Scene in San Francisco after the 1906 fire . . . . *facing* 126

A train stops at "Miller's Retreat" . . . . *following* 126

North Shore train overturned by earthquake in 1906 . . . *following* 126

North Pacific Coast No. 21 at Sausalito . . . . *following* 126

North Pacific Coast train at Howard's . . . . *following* 126

"The Battle of Sebastopol Avenue" . . . . *following* 126

Courthouse Square, Santa Rosa, in the '80s . . . . . . *following* 126

Courthouse Square, Santa Rosa, in 1909 . . . . *following* 126

The "Big White Cars" at Sebastopol, 1909 . . . . . . *following* 126

Wreck on the Petaluma & Santa Rosa Railroad . . . . . *following* 126

Train at Monte Rio in 1913 . . . . *following* 126

Boarding the train at Guernewood Park . . . . *following* 126

Healdsburg Station in 1908 . . . . *following* 126

Virginia & Truckee Locomotive I. E. JAMES buried in slide *following* 126

Train at Camp Meeker in 1910 . . . . *following* 126

Narrow Gauge "boneyard" at Point Reyes . . . . *following* 126

Santa Fe cross on Eureka Depot, 1904 . . . . *following* 126

Island Mountain . . . . *following* 126

Train of ex-narrow gauge coaches in San Rafael . . . . . *following* 126

Electric cars at San Anselmo . . . . *following* 126

Mt. Tamalpais & Muir Woods Railway train at Mill Valley *following* 126

North Shore electric car . . . . *following* 126

Northwestern Pacific electric train near Escalle . . . . . *following* 126

Interior of North Shore electric car . . . . *following* 126

Gold Spike Special at Sausalito . . . . *following* 126

Northwestern Pacific president driving golden spike . . . *following* 126

Inspection car in 1908 . . . . *following* 126

Train No. 21 at Preston . . . . *following* 126

Train at Sherwood in 1908 . . . . *following* 126

Northwestern Pacific locomotive 227 at Tiburon . . . . *following* 126

Passenger locomotive No. 52 . . . . *following* 126

The Sausalito ferry slips . . . . *facing* 127

Fort Seward . . . . *facing* 127

MAPS IN POCKET AT END OF BOOK:

Ferry and rail routes of the North Pacific Coast Railroad between San Francisco and Saucelito, San Quentin and San Rafael.

Map from Northwestern Pacific employees timetable at about the time the road was operating over the greatest number of miles of track.

Redwood Railways

Orientation map for Chapter I showing location of Petaluma & Haystack R.R. as reached by steamer from San Francisco.

I

The Cows and Chickens Line

IT WAS the morning of August 27, 1866. John A. McNear, leading citizen of Petaluma, was going to San Francisco. He strode down B Street from his office to the depot, amused but a little annoyed. For his young son George had just staged a pretty tantrum on being forbidden to go along to see the choo-choo.

The train, McNear noticed, had been made up differently from the usual custom. Normally the little five-ton Atlas locomotive pushed her train down to the steamer landing, but today, except for a leading box car, the engine stood at the head end. Coupled behind her was a flat car loaded with chicken coops, followed by a baggage car and a coach, the latter inside the station canopy.

Some of the passengers, preferring to ride outside in the balmy morning air, had seated themselves on the chicken coops and John McNear joined them.

The Petaluma & Haystack Railroad had been running a little over two years. It was part of the operations of Charles Minturn, known around San Francisco Bay as the "ferryboat king." His Contra Costa Steam Navigation Company, however, was losing its monopoly on the Eastbay crossing, and Minturn had looked to the north shore to maintain the volume of his business.

For in the early sixties the country north of San Francisco—Marin, Sonoma, and southern Mendocino—was largely a land of spreading wheat farms, the universal California harvest. Here and

1

there the specialty crops that would soon crowd out the wheat were in infant stages of development—the orchards, vineyards and hop fields, the poultry farms and dairies. The redwoods that had once reached to the very waters of the Bay had been used to build the City. The groves in the Russian River country had just begun to hear the ringing axes that meant they were to follow. In between, the whole region was liberally studded with tiny hamlets gravely regarding themselves as towns and cities. Each was fairly self-sufficient, and had to be, because before Charlie Minturn came along, transportation was almost nonexistent.

Even crossing the Bay from San Francisco had not been lightly undertaken. You could take passage on a schooner bound for Corte Madera del Presidio where lumber for the original Spanish army post was cut, and perhaps get across in a couple of hours. Or, if winds and tides were hostile, it might take days. The Union Packet line ran up the creek to Petaluma and carried mostly hay. A few little brigs scudded outside the heads and served the coastal hamlets. That was all.

Minturn had eyed this situation and cased the growing towns of Petaluma and San Rafael. In 1860 he started a steamboat up Peta-luma Creek to Lakeville. Here one could climb aboard a stage and be jounced seven miles to Petaluma, or the many, many more aching miles to Santa Rosa and Ukiah—or even back to San Rafael!

Which last situation had evoked howls of anguish from the few hundred residents of Marin's county seat, who could look across the Bay and see San Francisco, but who could not see any reason why they should have to reach it by circumnavigation. So Minturn opened his San Quentin ferry to serve them. This in itself could hardly be promoted as rapid transit, although the Rafaelites had joyously crowded the little Point San Quentin wharf when the first boat warped in.

The fare was two dollars but you got your money's worth in mileage. Leaving San Francisco, the ferry headed for the Contra Costa shore and made three or four ports of call — discharged a passenger or two, loaded a few cases of butter or maybe a wild steer. Then it droned west again to tie up at San Quentin some four hours later. Still it was better than the lumber schooners.

In the meantime the Petaluma Creek service flourished. Actually, it was not a creek but a meandering slough with fifty changes of course and thirteen foot spring tides to contend with, and expert navigation was required. Until Minturn dredged out a channel to Haystack Landing, the little *Petaluma* was often stranded in the tules.

This was not the only improvement that he planned, and in April of 1862 the Sacramento solons approved his franchise for a railway from Petaluma to the Landing. No competing line, the charter provided, could ever be built within 400 feet of his track.

Two years later growing traffic justified the project. In March of 1864 muckers were busily grading from Petaluma southward to Italian Garden. And in San Francisco the Atlas Foundry began work on Minturn's order for a $5000 locomotive designed to develop all of twenty-six horsepower.

On August first Charles Minturn opened the Petaluma & Haystack Railroad to the public. The town fathers had turned down his bid to use the City Plaza as a depot, and he had had to be content with a small plot at First and B Streets. There was no particular fanfare about the opening—the Ferryboat King was never a man for frills. But the little three-mile railroad with the rural name had immediately assumed an important place in the life of Petaluma.

The poultry capital, already the largest town in Sonoma County, assumed metropolitan airs. Stage coaches and freight wagons clustered around the station, for Minturn quite naturally built no wagon road to his new steamer landing. Travelers for Santa Rosa and north were saved a stop-over in town by Hinkle's Night Coach which connected with the train. Petaluma felt itself permanently established as the "Head of Navigation."

Two years later Minturn extended his track southward to Rudesill's landing, reducing his steamer mileage. Still the rails were a long way short of Black Point where his franchise allowed him to go.

But to get back to the train on which John McNear and some others perched on chicken coops stacked on the open flat car. At eight o'clock Captain Warner of the *Petaluma,* who also doubled in brass buttons as conductor of the train, yelled "all aboard!"

Engineer Joe Levitt yanked his whistle cord and tardy passengers hastened to the cars, vaguely wondering why the blast sounded unusually shrill. Joe had been running locomotives for twenty years, most recently on the San Francisco & San Jose. They had been first class engines, too, he had remarked to a few Petalumans, not dinky coffee-pots like this home-made wonder. He had agreed to handle it for just a few days while Minturn searched for an "engineer of inferior grade at less wages" to replace his regular man who'd quit.

Perhaps Levitt had daydreamed himself back in the cab of one of those giants of the rails and was therefore unconcerned when the steam gauge hit 120 pounds with no popping off — the safety valve should have let go at 80. Or perhaps he had forgotten that the frugal Minturn provided no fireman and that he was also responsible for the water level in the boiler. A frantic cry from the station agent brought him back to earth — but only for his last moment on it.

A flash, a dull heavy roar, the hiss of imprisoned steam in sudden berserk freedom, and the air was full of flying pistons, twisted boiler tubes, fractured drivers, and other sad fragments of the Atlas engine's anatomy. Levitt, bloody and mangled, lay dying on the rails several hundred feet down the track. Atop the baggage car, itself blown up against the depot, sprawled two corpses—one minus a head. Other bodies lay still where the blast had blown them, or where flying metal had laid them low.

McNear, on his chicken coop, had bent to knot a shoelace. As he straightened, a chunk of iron hurtled by, and he thanked the Lord he'd kept his son at home. Then the townsfolk came running, and he and the conductor-captain took charge and restored some order to the shambles.

Most of the passengers had been inside the cars and were uninjured. Warner sent sixty of them in horse-drawn coaches to the

Petaluma which departed with the mate in command. Volunteers gave first aid to the injured and the four dead were reverently carried from the scene.

Bad as it was, the catastrophe could have been much worse had the boiler exploded two minutes sooner when most of the passengers were still on the platform, or had the train been made up in the usual custom with the locomotive at the rear inside the entrance to the station.

The Petaluma & Haystack Railroad was now sans motive power. Minturn announced at once that he'd order another locomotive, but nothing ever came of it. Instead, the Petalumans soon noticed workmen fitting up the P. & H. rolling stock with shafts and whiffle-trees. Others were filling the track smooth and level between the rails. For the balance of its history the Petaluma & Haystack operated with the four-legged type of horsepower.

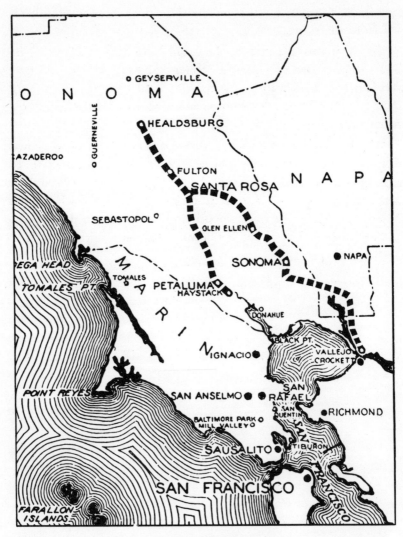

Orientation map for Chapter II showing proposed locations of railroads in Napa and Sonoma Counties.

II

The Battle of the Paper Railroads

THE PEOPLE of Petaluma and the rest of Sonoma County craved a real railroad. But soon they were torn between this desire and the fear that they might get one they didn't want. Twenty-five miles eastward, the Napa Valley Railroad was being built northward from Vallejo, and Petalumans had nightmares in which they saw it extended from Calistoga to the Russian River country, leaving their fair city to wither on the vine. On the other hand, they felt a proper railway should go no further south — Petaluma must remain the "head of navigation," and when, in February of 1865, a rumor got around that Lakeville Landing was being eyed as a prospective through railroad terminal, the Petaluma *Argus* wailed that this would leave the egg city a consumptive skeleton.

Nothing much really happened for quite a while, however. In October, the Petaluma & Healdsburg Railroad Company was organized by the bigwigs of those towns and Santa Rosa. C. W. Langdon of the latter place was president; I. G. Wickersham, Petaluma banker, the treasurer; and John McMannis of Healdsburg, secretary. Between them they couldn't have raised enough cash to buy a single locomotive, and their project died in maternity with each town blaming both the others for the demise. Railroad talk, however, cost nothing, and there was plenty of it to come.

By the close of 1867, jaws were wagging furiously throughout Sonoma County. There were two big issues and a four-way split in public opinion: (1) Should the connection with San Francisco be

7

via Petaluma or Vallejo? and (2) Should a county subsidy be offered? The further north one traveled the more folks seemed to favor Vallejo — to the amazed disgust of Petaluma. "Nature," explained the *Argus,* "has planned the route through this country, and to run from Healdsburg to Vallejo would simply be an attempt to re-enact the laws of the Almighty." Which drew a horse laugh from the Healdsburg *Standard.* The *Argus* — "tadpole journal" of the "pollywog city" located "on a frog pond"— it described as proclaiming "in thunder tones that can be heard above the peeping of lizards, the croaking of frogs and the splashing of tadpoles: 'you have wallowed through the mud and mire for the last fifteen years to pay us tribute, and now how dare you talk of withdrawing your patronage!' " It was even alleged that Petaluma had sabotaged the railroad scheme of 1865, a charge that was obviously absurd.

The day after Christmas a meeting of aroused Petalumans adopted a charter some of them had prepared, for a second company to build a railroad to Healdsburg. This time they planned a branch to Bloomfield, a small hamlet fourteen miles northwest, as well. The name of the proposed road being left blank, a suggestion from the floor of "Sonoma County Railroad" was accepted. A $5,000 county subsidy for every mile was expected. These articles of incorporation were filed at Sacramento on the 10th day of January, 1868.

The Vallejo boys were not far behind. Led by John Frisbie, energetic banker son-in-law of old General Vallejo, the Vallejo & Sonoma Valley Railroad Company applied for its charter a few days later. Frisbie hoped to make Vallejo the main rail terminal of San Francisco Bay. He was building huge grain elevators there with which he hoped to overcome the California farmers' fixation on shipping his crop in sacks. This line through the sleepy old Mexican town of Sonoma and thence to Santa Rosa and Healdsburg would make the whole Russian River country and northward tributary to his port. Like the Petalumans, he also wanted a subsidy of $5,000 per mile from Sonoma County, if the Legislature agreed.

With these two competing projects before them, the state solons decided to pass the buck to the local voters. An election was set for the 12th of May at which time the questions of route and the $5,000 a mile subsidy would be decided.

This situation brought some rather important citizens into the picture. One was General Patrick Connor who had made a fortune in Utah mines. The general had broken trail down the Eel River Canyon back in '51 on his way to the Trinity River gold rush.

Here the oldest living wealth on earth had waited for the Americans. The Spaniards, in three centuries, had hardly stirred themselves to investigate its borders. The Russians had puttered around with a little beachhead for a few years, but couldn't make it pay. As for the original denizens, how would a Hoopa Indian have felled a giant redwood tree?

The general had never forgotten those quiet, endless files of virgin redwoods, their ruddy bark dim as the sun's rays slid down on the lifting fog. And so we find him, early in 1868, with Fred McCrellish, publisher of the San Francisco *Alta,* and John F. Mc-Cauley, a promoter with an "in" at Sacramento, pushing a franchise through the Legislature for a railroad from Saucelito to Humboldt Bay.

With government subsidy, a railroad through Sonoma County and on to the north could be a very attractive speculation while, even with this assistance, much too costly for local capital to swing. It seemed an opportunity for a man with means and knowledge of the untapped wealth that awaited transportation. On March 2, 1868, Connor and his associates McCauley and McCrellish, incorporated the San Francisco & Humboldt Bay Railroad Company for $8,600,000. McCrellish had also induced Frederick A. Bee to join the group. A forty-niner, Bee had played a large part in conceiving and putting over both the Pony Express and the first overland telegraph. Recently he had been president of the Sacramento & Placerville Railroad. He was a most valuable man, though regarded with some suspicion because he advocated a square deal for the Chinese.

Meanwhile, supporters of the two rival routes beat the drums all over Sonoma County. Mass meetings were whooped up in the remotest hamlets — Bodega Corners, Freestone, Duncan's Mill — and the will of Providence for one line or the other was clearly demonstrated; the sly knavery of those promoting the alternative exposed through the powers of elocution. Petaluma, fighting for her life she felt, led off with an all-out rally. Bonfires blazing on downtown corners, clanging firebells, and a fife and drum corps that tootled its way all over town mobilized a record-breaking crowd. McCune's Hall couldn't handle it, and the affair had to be moved to Hinshaw's much larger auditorium, itself soon jammed to the rafters.

President Joe Cutter of the Sonoma County Railroad Company took the chair. His outfit, he said, was an honest company with an honest name. It proposed to build a railway from Petaluma to Cloverdale through Santa Rosa and Healdsburg — almost a straight line. There would be a branch to Bloomfield. For this sixty miles of track a donation of $300,000 from the county was justified and expected. The "pretended purpose" of Frisbie's company, he went on, was to build from Vallejo through Sonoma Valley to Santa Rosa and on to Cloverdale, with a Bloomfield branch — eighty-eight miles. But the real diabolical scheme of the Vallejo slickers, honest Petalumans were warned, was to build only sixteen miles to Healdsburg from the Calistoga terminal of the Napa Valley Railroad, then claim to have completed a railway from Vallejo to Healdsburg, and demand $5,000 in good Sonoma County bonds for each of the forty-one miles of it.

Connor's San Francisco & Humboldt Bay Railroad Company was represented by Colonel Bee, who said in effect, "when your subsidy is approved, endorse it over to us and we'll build your road in eight months." Five hundred Petalumans signed a resolution which was offered: namely, that a railroad be built from Saucelito to Cloverdale. Two years before they had been adamant against their town becoming a "way station." The Vallejo bogey had scared them, and with good reason, for Mr. Jackson Temple, president of the Vallejo & Sonoma Valley Railroad Company and a most persuasive speaker (he was later Supreme Court Justice), was packing the halls throughout northern Sonoma County and fast selling a bill of goods for Frisbie.

Election night, May 12th, saw anxious crowds clustered around the office of the Petaluma *Argus*. The local returns came in first, of course — 669 to 1 for the Sonoma County Railroad. Had the lone subversive been discovered, it is likely that tar would have been put to heating and pillows gutted of their feathers. Santa Rosa and Healdsburg gave Frisbie's route large majorities, but when the county totals were in, the Petaluma route had won 2095 to 1586. In the poultry capital, the hens were kept awake that night by triumphant cannons firing in the plaza. The subsidy, to go to whichever road won, was approved everywhere.

On the Glorious Fourth, the directors of the Sonoma County Railroad gathered before the Revere House at the head of Main Street in Petaluma and "broke ground." This ceremony marked the beginning and end of construction under their auspices. A few days later they met again and accepted Bee's proposal, transferring all their rights to the San Francisco & Humboldt Bay Railroad Company, but providing for recapture unless ten miles of track were completed by November 19, 1869. Feeling their duties well discharged, they relaxed at the big camp meeting around the corner where Reverends Loughborough and Bourdeaux were expounding on "Fulfillment of Prophecy."

ASBURY HARPENDING AT 16

from an early photograph

III

The Boy Wonder

THE SAN FRANCISCO & HUMBOLDT BAY RAILROAD COMPANY had not stood still in the few months of its corporate life. General Connor already had a preliminary line surveyed, starting at Saucelito, skirting the western shore of Richardson's Bay on the way to San Rafael, and thence as far as Petaluma. He had established ferry service to Saucelito with the little side-wheel steamer *Princess* on May 10, 1868. Near the landing, a dance platform had been knocked together and some town lots laid out.

But Connor, McCrellish and McCauley together did not have the kind of money needed to build their railroad — even with the subsidy. That would just about pay for the rails. They had, of course, known that from the beginning and figured that when they had the franchise, capital could be found. And Fred McCrellish now found it — in the pockets of a man who, had he lived a few decades later, would almost certainly have been known as the Boy Wonder.

Asbury Harpending was a gold seeker who arrived in California very late — 1857. However, he couldn't have very well made it much sooner, as he was still only sixteen. A good-looking, black-haired Kentucky lad, brimming with enthusiasm, daring, and a latent touch of Midas, he had been well supplied with funds for the voyage west from the parental purse, but his nest egg was in Kentucky state currency and almost worthless at New Orleans where he embarked. Only five dollars jingled faintly in his pockets after the humiliating purchase of a steerage ticket — this he nonchalantly ran up to several hundred by auctioning off the purser's fruit supply as soon as the ship sailed. Then he moved to a first class cabin and arrived in San Francisco with a good stake.

Thereafter Harpending continued to go first class. Though others found the gold fields played out, young Asbury had the happy knack of coming along just as a group of experienced miners gave up as worthless a claim on which they had spent much cash and sweat, working it a little deeper and cleaning up. Age seventeen found him with $60,000. Two years in Mexico followed. Then he had sailed back through the Golden Gate, owning a quarter of a million in cold cash and a Sonora mine worth a million more, but still too young to vote.

A few days later, Lincoln was elected and secession started. Harpending, an ardent Southerner, plunged himself and his bankroll into deep-laid plots to make California a Confederate state, schemes that just barely missed success. Almost evenly divided loyalties characterized the new state so far from Washington. The Southern underground, including many prominent Californians whose names still remain undisclosed behind their oaths of secrecy, planned a coup d'etat. Young Asbury spent his time and dollars freely in the cause but the putsch was called off. Deeply disappointed, he went East, served a few days on General Beauregard's staff at the battle of Shiloh and then was handed a captain's commission in the Confederate Navy by Jefferson Davis, although he had never even been aboard a warship.

Captain Harpending soon stood on the deck of his first command, a Confederate cruiser, anchored in San Francisco Bay! No one knew she was a cruiser but he and his brother officers who had just bought the ex-clipper. None among them were sailors, so they had to hire a navigator who promptly gave away the show. The Confederate "naval officers" found themselves lodged on Alcatraz, charged with high treason, and soon convicted of it. Harpending was released after four months on The Rock. Almost immediately he was warned of

Minturn's ferry *Contra Costa* at Green Street Wharf in San Francisco, 1869

Charles Minturn's ferry landing at San Quentin in the '60s.

Train from San Quentin approaching San Rafael after conversion of the S.R. & S.Q. to narrow gauge by the North Pacific Coast.

plans to rearrest him. Now flat broke, he hid out in the foothills back of Fresno, stumbled onto another mine, and salted away $800,000. Then, the war being over and by-gones considered by-gones, he reappeared in San Francisco and became a large scale operator in real estate.

The extension of Montgomery Street, then the main artery of the city, across Market became his pet project, and he began quietly buying up lots where the new thoroughfare would have to go. William C. Ralston, financial genius of the Bank of California, guessed what Harpending was about, and eased himself into the scheme. They laid out New Montgomery Street for two blocks through their aggregate purchased parcels and were confidently expecting to continue it to the Bay.

Such was the young man Fred McCrellish sought to interest in the San Francisco & Humboldt Bay Railroad. The publisher must have been amazed at his own success — possibly it exceeded both his expectations and desires. For Asbury Harpending, infected with the railroad bug like most Californians as the Central Pacific neared completion, took over 90 per cent of the deal after a very sketchy investigation. General Connor and McCrellish he bought out completely — of the original franchise holders only John McCauley, useful as a front man and lobbyist, remained.

The young Kentucky wonder now plunged into railroad promotion with his usual impetuous energy and enthusiasm. Astride a horse, he traced out the whole route, marvelled at the unhomesteaded redwood forests along the Eel River, and gloated over visions of Congressional railroad land grants through such a country. Why, he asked himself, had he been wasting his time with gold mines?

Soon he had Colonel Bee out with several grading gangs and dirt was flying. He ordered fifty miles of ties and the same amount of rail—some of it from Peter Donahue's Union Iron Works in San Francisco and the rest from England. But Ralston refused to have anything to do with the project. Incredibly, for a man so obsessed with California's possibilities, the banker regarded the north coast counties as only "fit for coyotes." But this worried Harpending not at all—it never occurred to him to doubt his own ability, financial and otherwise, to build the road and make it pay rich dividends. He sent Pat Connor to Washington to lobby for a land grant.

Harpending's plans expanded. He talked of a magnificent suspension bridge across the Golden Gate that would carry his trains right into San Francisco. There would be a massive oval pier in the center of the strait, connected with each shore by 2,000-foot spans carrying double tracks 175 feet above the water. Atop the center anchorage would be a towering lighthouse and on each of the shore abutments revolving monitor turrets for Coast Artillery cannons. This was ambitious dreaming for 1868 when the 1,000-foot Cincinnati bridge was the longest in the world. Seventy years later, a single 4,200-foot suspension span would cross the Gate but the Oakland bridge with its center anchorage and two 2,300-foot spans 185 feet high would surprisingly resemble Harpending's plans of '68.

Grading continued north of Petaluma through the fall and winter. Colonel Bee and McCauley both went on record that trains would run to Santa Rosa by January first. But when the Petalumans gathered at their big New Year's Ball, their wives and daughters in high style "Grecian Bends" and pale from chewing chalk with arsenic for a milky skin, the only trains around were still Minturn's oat burners. Grading continued through the winter but at a reduced tempo as Harpending was becoming short of cash.

Up around Healdsburg, folks were still suspicious of anything starting at Petaluma, and cracker barrel gossip agreed the "earth scratching" was just a vaccination to ward off a railroad.

At the annual stockholders' meeting in January, Harpending installed Judge Solomon Heydenfeldt as president, Assemblyman John Romer, secretary, and retained the post of treasurer for himself. McCauley and Captain Harrison, still in charge of affairs at Saucelito, were directors.

By March, the roadbed was graded within three miles of Santa Rosa and the bridge over Petaluma Creek was under way. Fifteen miles of iron had sailed from England. Ties began to arrive. And bills, too. Harpending was finding railroad building more expensive than he'd figured. He needed cash in large quantities and arranged with Ralston to auction their New Montgomery Street properties, expecting thus to realize a couple of million dollars. However, Ralston's usual overconfident optimism set the minimum bids too high; despite well staged hot bidding everything was knocked down to their own shills, and the auction was a fizzle. A few days later, work was suspended on the San Francisco & Humboldt Bay Rail Road.

Consternation and confusion followed. John McCauley, who had to close down the job and lay off the men, was made the goat in the public press. Judge Heydenfeldt resigned, and Harpending made McCauley president. The new chief brightened the situation but feebly by the gesture of resuming work on the Petaluma Creek bridge.

The driving of the gold spike at Promontory in May touched off a recession in San Francisco as many believed that the transcontinental railroad would lessen the importance of the port. Harpending continued to have difficulty in liquidating his real estate, and it was four months before work on the roadbed could be resumed. By this time McCauley was in the East shopping for cars and locomotives. Then came word that the shipment of English rails lay at the bottom of Valparaiso harbor in the hold of a sunken bark. By agreement, unless the S.F. & H.B. could show ten miles of completed track by the 19th of November, its rights and roadbed would revert to the Sonoma County Railroad Company. No rails being locally available, the condition obviously could not be met.

But three days before the deadline Harpending organized the San Francisco and North Pacific Rail Road Company with almost the same directors. With this new corporation he wangled another contract from the Sonoma County people.

Undaunted by these details, the youthful promoter's dreams had now expanded to visualize a far-flung railroad empire. Pat Connor's Washington lobbying for federal redwood land grants had not paid off, so he was working for State grants of salt marsh and tide lands around San Francisco Bay. Assemblyman Romer introduced the bill; it would present Harpending's railroad company with 3,625 acres— 200 in San Francisco's North Beach section and the balance in Marin, including nine miles of water front and all of Richardson's Bay. Not to seem too modest, a gift of $300,000 from Marin County was likewise provided for. The area would have made a wonderful railroad terminal, but traffic from the northwestern counties alone, it seemed certain, would never justify such enormous facilities.

Actually, the ex-Confederate captain was now thinking in terms of a second transcontinental. He had learned of the North Fork Feather River route — undiscovered in the days of Judah — that made Beckwourth Pass, for grade and snow, far superior to the Central Pacific's route across the Sierras. He had secured control of the Oroville & Virginia City Railroad, a local outfit in the paper stage with a quarter million dollar disputed subsidy and a large land grant bill in Congress. He had hired General Rosecrans and Arthur W. Keddie to survey a line between Oroville and the route of the San Francisco & North Pacific. Now he had a small gang of Chinamen actually grading in the Feather River Canyon.

In Sacramento, Romer and McCauley put the heat on the tidelands bill, the former from his vantage point in an Assembly seat, the latter in his "ranch" on the corner of 5th and K, where popping champagne corks and other entertainment provided a pleasant background for solonic discussions. But soon they realized that Harpending had been too greedy. A loud howl arose against the "land grant." A Marin shore farmer voiced the views of many:

> "We could stand land grabbing by itself and we could endure Emperor Norton for a little while by himself. But excuse us; these gentlemen of the San Francisco and North Pacific, North Pole, Northern Siberia, North Great Central, Open Sea Railroad are too overpowering, too grand, too magnificent in their conceptions. They have only one fault — they are too modest? Poor little Marin! What a pity there is not a little more meat on your precious bones! Well, never mind, they will take the rest in cash! We have saved up a little butter money, and we have raised some little cows and

calves, and after taking all the land we have, and inasmuch as the cows and calves are not convenient for gentlemen to carry off with them, they will just quietly tap us for $300,000."

With considerable pressure and lavish "entertaining," McCauley and Romer got their bill through Assembly, but the Senate was less susceptible and killed it without a hearing.

The Central Pacific people agreed with the Marin coast rancher —Harpending was too grand! They were not concerned about whatever he might do 'way up in the sticks of Humboldt and Mendocino, but when he looked toward the Sierras and beyond, California became too small for both concerns. The Kentuckian and his cohorts had been adept at "pressure" — now they found themselves on the receiving end. The rails ordered from Peter Donahue were still withheld — no others were available on the coast. The grapevine had it that the ship sunk in Valparaiso had actually been scuttled. Unforeseen roadblocks arose in every quarter. Finally the Big Four worked on Harpending through William Ralston. The banker had helped the C.P. through its construction days; he had expected to receive the car building concession in return and had built the Kimball factory for that purpose. But now word came to him, he could get his former partner out of the railroad business or expect war instead of contracts.

Asbury Harpending was extremely loath to quit. Long odds had never worried him much. But he had acquired a great affection for Ralston. Then too, the banker could help him sell the S.F. & N.P. at a worthwhile profit. So he agreed to get out — a decision that may have had great bearing on the course of events in the West. For it is just possible that the boy wonder could have carried out his dreams — that what is now the Western Pacific would have been built four decades sooner, and with its terminal at Sausalito.

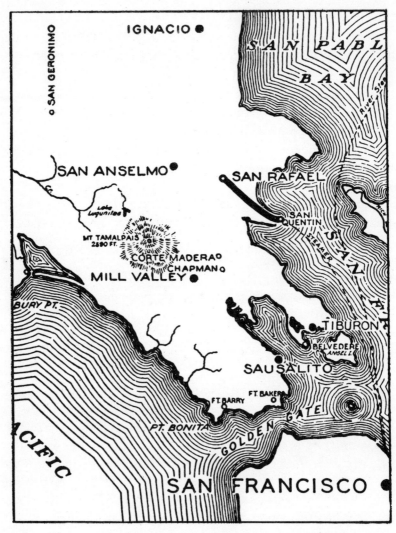

Orientation map for Chapter IV showing location of San Rafael & San
Quentin R.R. as reached by steamer from San Francisco.

IV

The Commuter is Born

IN THE MEANTIME, the folks of quiet little San Rafael had quietly built a little railroad. Tranquillity had been the habit of this peaceful village ever since the Franciscans built their mission early in the century — a repose completely shattered once a year when visitors flocked in to help celebrate the birthday of its patron saint. Sheltered by Mount Tamalpais from the clammy fogs of San Francisco, its climate and suburban beauty had drawn many prosperous families who were enthralled with the place and wished to keep it just as it was. As one gushing Rafaelite put it:

> "Like a beautiful maiden sitting at the feet of her betrothed, and with wistful eyes looking into the face of him she loves, or like a devotee to knowledge gazing up the steep acclivity of the hill of science, longing for the time when he shall overcome the difficulties in his path of knowledge, or shall gain the goal of his aspirations, so nestles San Rafael at the foot of Tamalpais—so coy and demure that a lover of the beautiful, in gazing upon the scene, cannot help but admire the picture, and he is not surprised that the dwellers therein are proud of their village and its surroundings."

But they were not proud of the way they had to reach it. True, Charlie Minturn now ran ferries to Point San Quentin, but at the wharf one must climb into a creaky stagecoach with "Sweet William" Adams at the ribbons and jounce about an hour over an appalling "road" along the summit of the ridge to San Rafael. Fare from San Francisco: Ferry, $2.00; Stage, a dollar more.

21

After a couple of years of ferry service, a turnpike was built across the marsh. The east bay ports of call were eliminated, fares were cut in half, and the running time slashed to a neat two hours. Still the service had its rough spots. Like the time Minturn found a cut-rate captain and fired the popular young John McKenzie from the run — he was always looking for cheap help, if you recall the Petaluma episode. The cheap captain lacked the skill to land one morning when the Bay was a trifle choppy and a score of commuters waited on the wharf. Finally he sent the mate ashore in a small boat and picked up five of them. The others, waiting for their turn, gasped in astounded fury when they saw the ferry calmly steam away, leaving them to slosh back to town on foot as the stage driver had been one of the lucky five. A few days later, most of San Rafael had signed a petition that convinced Mr. Minturn he would be wise to reinstate Captain McKenzie.

The commuters, of which even then there were quite a few, grew very weary of the stagecoach and its alternative — riding their own horses to the Point and tying them up in the stable. Coming home evenings on the *Contra Costa,* in a deck corner sheltered from the trade winds sweeping in the Gate, they began to talk railroad. James D. Walker and Sidney V. Smith took the lead and the conversations culminated January 12, 1869 in a mass meeting that jammed the old mission era 'dobe of Don Timoteo Murphy, now used as the county court house. Smith acted as chairman and a committee of nine was chosen to dig into costs, right of way problems and the like. Within a month, the San Rafael and San Quentin Railroad Company was organized as a $50,000 corporation. More than a third of the stock was subscribed before the ink was dry.

Adolph Mailliard was chosen president, a man of unusual background. Born in New Jersey, he had been brought up in France and at eighteen was secretary to Joseph Bonaparte, deposed King of Spain. On Bonaparte's death, he became executor of the will. He had come to California for his health and bought the 6,500-acre Rancho San Geronimo at White's Hill, some ten miles northwest of San Rafael.

Now, at sixty again full of vigor, he was one of the town's leading citizens.

Early March saw surveyors wading through the salt marshes. Cost of the railroad had been estimated at $40,000 complete with rolling stock — by no means expensive as railroads go, but even so the last few thousands were pretty hard to get. The directors had to threaten to junk the whole project before all the stock was taken late in April. Most of the right-of-way was donated but some had to be condemned, notably a parcel owned by John McCauley who quickly proved his skill on the unfamiliar side of the fence by collecting $50 an acre for salt marsh assessed at about a dollar. A lot at the foot of B Street was donated for a depot site, and the company was ready to receive bids to build and equip the road.

The low bid was Ezekial White's — $24,000 in gold. Soon his gang of black-pajamaed Chinamen were wielding picks and wheelbarrows and driving piles in the marsh. They worked one week and then they struck! Eleven hour day too muchee, ten hour day muchee better! After some palaver they agreed to work eleven hours for another month, then to switch to ten. This was satisfactory with Zeke — he expected to have the whole roadbed done by then.

Came San Rafael Day, Saturday, October 23rd, and with it the annual invasion of hard characters from the City. Minturn placed an extra steamer on the run and both ferries were jammed. Along Fourth Street three-card monte sharps and shell game artists began separating yokels from their hard-earned cash at an early hour. A brass band blared on the Court House lawn, and countless hawkers peddled oranges, peanuts and pineapples through the crowds milling around in the hot, dusty sunshine. Whiskey could be bought most anywhere and was swigged in amazing volume. Night fell. The hotels had been sold out for weeks, but few cared for no one wanted to sleep. No one could — downtown. The Rafaelites, for the most part, stayed in their secluded homes and watched over their valuables, wondering why they put up with this yearly fracas.

Sunday was the bullfight, and fresh hordes poured over on the
Contra Costa. At two o'clock, three none-too-expert matadors appeared in the packed bull ring at Second and B; flaunted their
dazzling costumes and red *capas* before a bored "bull" who yesterday
had been hauling logs on Mount Tamalpais; then scaled the side of
the arena in panic when he woke up enough to get annoyed. The
"great Senor Golindo" then took over, made a few passes with his
muleta to induce the bull to charge and watched the seat of his pants
depart, impaled on the zooming horns. So unnerved was the great
toreador at the exposure of his underwear that had a spectator not
jumped into the ring and saved him, the bull would probably have
finished him off. Those of Castillian blood in the howling mob shud-
dered at the fiasco.

That night Fourth Street was a complete bedlam until dawn —
yelling, hooting drunks, a pair of tipsy bagpipe tootlers, and a far
from sober German band combined in pandemonium better read
about than heard. Over in Short's Assembly Hall, the local celebrants
had to strain their ears to keep step with the music at their sedate
St. Raphael's Birthday Ball. Monday and Tuesday were much the
same. Professor Winn and his troupe of trained pigs appeared in
town, providing a new fillip. They should have felt right at home.
Fights came oftener and red-eye still flowed in volume. But there is a
limit to human endurance, and on Wednesday the bleary crowds
began to drift down to the ferry. By Thursday San Rafael "Day"
was over and tranquillity reigned again. The Rafaelites cleaned up
the mess, resumed the quiet order of their lives and the building of
their railroad.

Early in December the roadbed was finished and the bark *Wen-
nington* arrived from Liverpool with rails. January saw them spiked
down despite stormy weather. A small locomotive boasting the name
of "San Rafael" was delivered from San Francisco but wouldn't per-
form and had to be returned for overhauling.

Sunday morning, March 20th, 1870, the "San Rafael" and her
one car train were displayed to admiring crowds by Superintendent

David Nye at the B Street depot. Regular service started the next day at 7:45 a.m. Few spectators watched because of the early hour and yesterday's inspection, but inside the little coach two solid lines of commuters faced each other on the lengthwise wooden seats. Engineer Covert gently pulled his throttle open and started something that was to endure for seventy-one years — commuting to Marin by rail and ferry.

At noon the little train puffed back, and now the whole town was there to see. It all looked quite metropolitan for a village of 700 souls. Stages, carriages, and express wagons parked around the station — even a wheelbarrow or two. San Rafael was becoming a city, folks told each other. Soon there would be gas mains and pipes from Lake Lagunitas instead of the three water carriers who trudged from door to door. Horse cars were even talked about and a new court house to replace Don Timoteo's old adobe.

Nye posted a schedule of two trips daily but it was soon jumped to three. Trains left San Rafael at 7:30 and 11:15 a.m. and 2:45 in the afternoon. Returning, the *Contra Costa* sailed from San Francisco at 9:30, 1:00 and 5:00.

The ride to the ferry took twelve minutes, but as Covert grew familiar with the "San Rafael's" possibilities he cut it down to seven. Fare was two bits and with the added traffic, Minturn cut the ferry rate to half a dollar, Mailliard bought a few flat cars to handle Sunday picnics. By July, the road was earning $600 a month. It was well appreciated by those who had for years piled atop the old stage coach or stowed away in its "boot." But memory is short, and only two years later the *Journal* was complaining: "(our) railroad (is) one of the most primitive in the country, the engine not having much more power than a donkey engine," and again, "cars . . . little better than second-rate immigrant—devoid of cushions, hot and close."

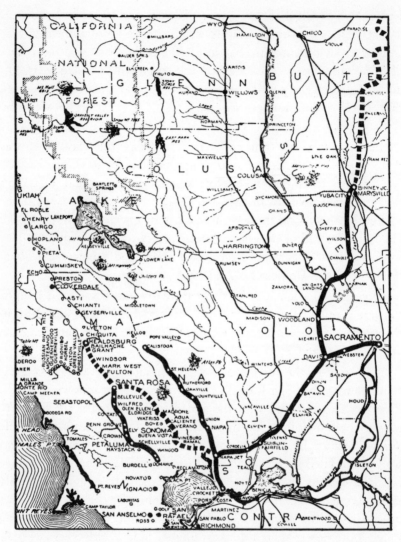

Orientation map for Chapter V showing the Cal. P. System and projected extensions at the pinnacle of its career.

26

V

Peter Donahue and the Cal. P.

To THE northward the railroad situation was still steaming. Local bigwigs, disgusted with the apparently inexcusable stalling of McCauley as he played the patsy for Harpending, organized the San Francisco and Northern Coast Railroad in February, 1870. The McNears of Petaluma purchased San Pedro Point, northeast of San Rafael, for its terminal, and the line was planned from there to Healdsburg, allowing it to qualify for the county subsidy. Among the incorporators was Colonel Bee, who had been spending his own money trying to speed Harpending's job but now had given up all hope in that direction.

The Vallejo crowd took heart again from Harpending's lack of action. Their town was now the terminal of the lusty California Pacific, running to Sacramento and Marysville and, since acquiring the Napa Valley Railroad, to Calistoga as well. Fast steamers linked it to San Francisco. They felt Vallejo had a fair chance to become the metropolis of the West. The Cal.P., as the road was called, had weathered a hard struggle following a very shaky start ten years before. But now it was in the hands of one of the dozen richest men in San Francisco, Milton Slocumb Latham — ex-governor, ex-senator, and ruler of the London and San Francisco Bank.

With his second bride, Latham occupied a Folsom Street mansion which squarely blocked the further extension of Harpending's New Montgomery Street project. Here all visiting artistic celebrities were

27

entertained and shown his own extensive art collections. From his office at the Bank, he directed a growing railway system that had the Big Four, just then in the throes of deciding to be a monopoly, more than a bit concerned. The Cal.P. now operated 163 miles of track, and although its financial position was not too steady, obviously it had ambitious plans in a good many directions. It was particularly humiliating to the Central Pacific moguls when their own transcontinental passengers got off at Sacramento and paid an extra fare on the Cal.P. to reach the City an hour and a half before their own round-about Stockton route would get them there.

The California Pacific delivered a definite proposal to the people of Sonoma County at a mass meeting in Santa Rosa, February 5, 1870. If a majority of the voters would sign a petition to the Legislature for a $300,000 subsidy to replace that granted to the Sonoma County Railroad, Cal.P. would build from Adelante (now Napa Junction) through the towns of Sonoma and Petaluma to Healdsburg, with the inevitable branch to Bloomfield. Further, if the petition could be qualified within a month, it promised twenty miles would be in operation before the end of December and twenty more each year to follow. The voters agreed and the Legislature approved.

Governor Haight finally pocket-vetoed this bill, but he did sign the General Railroad Law of 1870 which authorized county supervisors to submit proposals for donations of up to 5 per cent of assessed valuations to the voters. He had then executed a strange aboutface and declared the law was unconstitutional, but it was on the books, and the Sonoma supervisors decided to use it. They scheduled an election for June on the question of a $5,000 per mile subsidy to the first company completing ten miles of track. Then, to guard against being stuck for a double donation or having to subsidize track outside Sonoma County, they made a contract with Cal.P. agreeing, if the measure carried, to issue $25,000 in bonds on completion of the first five miles from the Napa County line. But they stipulated that if the S.F. & H.B. or its assigns the S.F. & N.P., or any other company managed to build a railroad through the county under the

Act of March 18, 1868, no bonds would be issued to Cal.P. unless the Vallejo road took it over.

The subsidy was victorious at the polls by a vote of 2-1. A few days later, Harpending completed a deal to sell the San Francisco & North Pacific to Peter Donahue, although the news of this did not leak out until the formal transfer was made August 2nd. Meanwhile, Latham had made continual, and of course fruitless, efforts to buy the graded roadbed from McCauley. Probably he was a bit upset when he discovered he had been bidding against a *fait accompli*.

But it was good news for Sonoma County. Peter Donahue had made a big success out of the San Francisco & San José after many others had failed, and it was just getting around that he had sold it to the Big Four of the Central Pacific. The supervisors felt so confident he would build their railroad that they ordered the bonds printed at once. Even so, they were a bit breathless at the speed with which Colonel Donahue moved in, after the endless futile grading of McCauley's gang. Over a hundred men were put to work—all white, for the Colonel would have no Chinese labor. The schooner-propeller *Twin Sister* shuttled up and down Petaluma Creek with ties, spikes and iron. Locomotives, cars and steamers were all ordered RUSH!, the former from Donahue's own Union Iron Works.

Peter Donahue was not a stranger to industry in action. Glasgow born, he was only eleven in 1833 when his family embarked for America, but he had already spent several years in the horrible child-labor sweatshops of the dawning Industrial Revolution. A few years later in New Jersey he was apprenticed to a machinist and in 1845 sailed for Peru on the maiden voyage of a gunboat which he had helped to build. There he might have stayed except for the cry of "GOLD" that echoed out of California and changed so many men's lives. The Fall of 1849 found him in San Francisco running a foundry in a tent. This flimsy enterprise he developed into the enormous Union Iron Works, one of the city's chief industries, turning out ships, mining machinery — and locomotives. From building engines it was an easy step to building railroads.

Donahue visited the job continually and conferred with Robert Harris, his superintendent; with Sonoma County District Attorney Overton, who would become the railroad's counsel, and with officials of the Hibernia Bank in San Francisco. He told the Petalumans that he intended to build south along the east side of the Creek to a temporary terminal near Lakeville but probably would eventually start his trains at Saucelito as Harpending had planned. In the meantime, the sidewheel river steamers *Sacramento* and *Wilson G. Hunt* were being refitted in the latest style and would plough up the Creek from San Francisco.

August 30th saw the first spike driven and only twelve days later the Petalumans enjoyed an excursion! A tiny construction locomotive had just been unloaded from the *Twin Sister,* and although there were no cars of any kind yet, when you're building a railroad you have an itch to ride on it. The Colonel told Bob Harris to pass out invitations and Petaluma's tycoonery clustered over the little engine like flies on a cook tent pie. Donahue was, of course, aboard, Bob Harris too, and Ed Fenton at the throttle. There was even a conductor, George W. Craig. Just before the take-off a ten-gallon keg of Edward's Cream Ale appeared and, despite the jam, room was found for it on the tender.

Fenton sounded a couple of squeaky blasts and the "train" started, moved over the bridge above Cinnabar Knoll, and covered the entire two miles of track. Some of the passengers seemed a bit nervous, probably recalling Minturn's ill-fated iron colt. But the dinky carried them all home safely, leaving only the empty keg behind.

The track went down rapidly on Harpending's grade. It would have gone down even quicker if the natives hadn't swarmed all over the construction trains, leaving little room for cargo. By the end of October it was complete except for ballasting, and the Supervisors, sagely examining the roadbed, issued bonds for the first ten miles. They were safe in doing so; it was all first class construction, 6″ x 8″ heart redwood ties and heavy T rail with fish joints.

Heald & Guerne Lumber Company's operations at Stumptown (now Guerneville). The locomotive was called BULLY BOY (not to be confused with the narrow-gauge BULLY BOY on the N.P.C.) but what the oxen were called was mostly unprintable.

When Peter Donahue took over the S.F. & N.P. project he brought the SAN JOSE (No. 2 of the San Francisco & San Jose Railroad) to be its first locomotive.

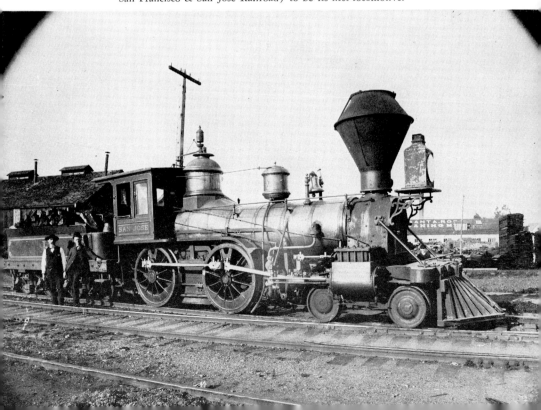

San Anselmo when it was known as "The Junction" in 1875. The N.P.C. main line, at that time, the track from San Quentin and San Rafael is on the other side of the depot. Red Hill in the distance.

N.P.C. Engine No. 4 OLEMA on the wood spur in Lagunitas Canyon sometime in the '80s.

The *Twin Sister* brought up the first passenger coach, a bright yellow beauty with her name "Lakeville" emblazoned in an oval on the side, with upholstered lengthwise seats for fifty people. This, of course, called for another excursion, and the dinky labored manfully to haul it and a flat car, both filled with road officials and Petalumans up to Santa Rosa. Superintendent Harris set up a bar in the "Lakeville" and with two assistant bartenders kept the champagne flowing and the crowd in rollicking spirits. There was never anything dry about one of Colonel Donahue's parties.

A week later the road had a real locomotive. Old No. 2, the "San Jose," from his former line became No. 1 of the San Francisco & North Pacific and went to work at once. Two more coaches arrived, the "Santa Rosa" and the "Petaluma" — all from Ralston's Kimball plant which had yet to see any Central Pacific orders. A palace car for the Colonel's private use, to surpass in luxury the best the East could offer, was also receiving the finishing touches there.

The first regular service on the S.F. & N.P. started October 31, 1870. The "San Jose," and her train left Petaluma at 8:00 a.m. and 1:30 p.m.; returned at noon and 4:00, the cars usually crowded. Santa Rosans gaped at all the hustle. The Fashion and California stages for up country moved their terminal from Petaluma; the town dandy, Ash Wilkinson, showed up with an omnibus and met all the trains. A public garden called "The Willows" was opened up for picnics. Run by the Philadelphia Brewery, it featured dancing, skating, shuffleboard and billiards, and, of course, light or dark on draught.

On the last day of 1870, Peter Donahue threw an excursion that showed up his previous ones for the local impromptu affairs they really were. Invitations went out to the elite of San Francisco. The *Sacramento,* they read, would leave Jackson Street wharf at 8:00 a.m. Some of the Colonel's friends had started to float the New Year in one night early and couldn't quite make this cockcrow departure; he held the boat for them, while Kidd's Brass Band and the Industrial School musicians alternately kept things humming. Company A of the California National Guard's First Artillery marched aboard, bringing a third band.

Fred McCrellish and John McCauley walked up the gang plank. With Pat Connor they had put through the original franchise and were surely entitled to some of the glory. Assemblyman Romer was there too, but Harpending had gone to London. William Tell Coleman, the old San Francisco Vigilante chief, appeared; back in California after many years in the East. Finally all were aboard and the *Sacramento* cast off; chuff-chuffed through the winter sunshine past Angel Island, San Quentin, and up Petaluma Creek. Aboard, the guests were dancing in the cabin (it was early morning, but why waste three bands?), indulging in mild steamer flirtations, or gabbing "railroad" between pick-me-ups. Soon the roar of artillery demanded their attention. They were at Donahue, the terminal of the railroad.

Ashore the "San Jose" stood steaming, behind her the three coaches and a dozen flats, all festooned with flags and evergreens. On one of the flat cars two field pieces from the National Guard Artillery were securely mounted. A salute of thirteen guns drowned out the "San Jose's" hissing cylinder cocks as the train, the Colonel and his guests all aboard, moved out of the new town he had built and given his name.

The Petaluma population greeted them with loud cheers. The Petaluma Guard, in full panoply, came to a smart "present arms"; then marched aboard the cars with other local guests. More cannon shots and the train was off again for Santa Rosa. Folks noticed that the track was smoother. It should have been — the grade had had two years to settle.

Santa Rosa was embarrassed! Somehow she had received no notice of the Inaugural Excursion, and only a vague rumor had drawn the crowd that clustered around end of track across the creek from town. They cheered and the feminine portion fluttered hankies, but what the 1,200 excursionists were thinking of was food! With only an hour stop-over planned, and vehicles not at hand, the famished visitors scampered down the road and across fields toward town to forage for eatables among the shops — all unprepared for such descending hordes.

Leaving the chagrined Santa Rosans, the still hungry party boarded the train for the return trip. Military formalities halted it for an hour in Petaluma. For the National Guard Battery marched in escort with the local troopers to their armory; some of the latter felt that etiquette of arms required them likewise to convoy their visitors back to the train — it was pointed out this might go on forever, so they compromised with some more salutes.

Back on the *Sacramento* a delectable smorgasbord with a staggering array of still and sparkling California wines explained the Colonel's omission of a spread at Santa Rosa. Then there were toasts and speeches as the ship snaked her way down Petaluma Creek. Coleman spoke in tribute to Donahue's performances — his amazingly swift construction, his exclusive use of white labor, the fact that his cars were local products, and that the Union Iron Works was building three locomotives which would join the "San Jose." The railroad president responded gracefully to the many kudos and added that all bills were paid; the road owed no man a dollar. Kidd's Band went into a mazurka, and the crowd danced back to San Francisco.

Next day — New Year's — regular service started from San Francisco through Donahue. The round house, machine shop, foundry and car sheds there were finished up; and a hotel, sporting water and gas in every room, opened to the travelling public. On the other end, Santa Rosa Creek was bridged and the permanent depot located on a seven-acre block between Third and Fourth, which cost $1,000. Construction continued north of the county seat — Healdsburg was the next objective. All appeared serene.

But the California Pacific was not out of the race. Its January stockholders' meeting voiced a strong urge to go ahead in Sonoma County regardless of Peter Donahue and his San Francisco & North Pacific. The English capitalists backing the London & San Francisco

Bank had insisted that Latham not start the new branch unless Vallejo would donate $100,000. Vallejo was not feeling that generous, so now its chief citizen, General Frisbie, made the required contribution personally in the interests of his beloved city. Cal.P. went into instant action.

Peter Donahue's Hibernian graders reported to the job one March morning and were all but stupefied to find a hundred pigtailed heathens busily building a parallel embankment. Cal.P. still had its contract for a subsidy, valid unless others built a railroad "through Sonoma County" first. The S.F. & N.P. already could be said to run "through" the county but did not extend from border to border. The ambiguity could pay off at $5,000 a mile, and the Marathon was on.

Donahue rushed more men to Santa Rosa. Latham countered with 200 Chinese reinforcements and started another party, 1,000 strong, on the route toward Napa. The Irish took advantage of the situation and walked off the job for higher pay. The Colonel swallowed his indignation and granted their demands to get them back. Latham shipped in still more Orientals and some Irish teamsters of his own. Cal.P. was covering a mile a day. Never had the somnolent countryside known such excitement, and local rooters cheered and placed their wagers. Every available man was thrown into the struggle, the rest of Donahue's railroad being so inactive that Santa Rosa urchins hitched stray nags to flat cars and rode up and down the track for hours.

Suddenly the battle was over. For a few days incredulous rumors flew; then the official word that Donahue had sold out to the California Pacific on April 13th. Ralston had stepped in again and convinced him that the only alternative was a well-heeled parallel competitor. As Harpending had, the Colonel took a nice profit out of the three-quarter million gold coin Latham paid.

The contract of sale provided that Donahue complete the line to Russian River so his Irish kept on working. The Chinamen, laid off, were intensely irritated, and the See Yup tong's paymaster was dis-

covered in the nick of time with a noose around his neck and a jab-
bering crowd of his countrymen about to hoist him to a tree. The
S.F. & N.P. was now the Petaluma and Humboldt Division of the
California Pacific. The Colonel's ex-employees presented him with
an elegant gold-handled cane and wondered what their new bosses
would be like.

Milton S. Latham now headed a very potent railroad system with
latent possibilities in no way inferior to those of the Central Pacific
itself. His new line was opened to Healdsburg July 1st. Almost simultaneously with the S.F. & N.P. acquisition, he purchased the Califor-
ia Steam Navigation Company operating on the Sacramento and San
Joaquin Rivers. The Cal.P. main stem from Vallejo to Sacramento
and Marysville was a basic artery. Now he incorporated the California Pacific Railroad Eastern Extension Company for $50,000,000
to build through Beckwourth Pass to a Union Pacific connection.
History was repeating itself speedily and with the same denouement.
Cal.P., the Big Four agreed, was indeed outgrowing its britches.

The Central Pacific crowd moved to attack throughout the summer. They gathered rail and ties for an air line route from Sacramento
to the Bay, shorter than the Cal.P. track. It would cut straight across
the tule marshes to Benicia. This terrain had been counted out by
everyone as a place where a man wacky enough to build a railroad
would see it promptly ooze into the tules, but Charles Crocker had
made test borings and knew he could get away with it. Stanford also
worked a few angles and came up with an exclusive franchise on the
Sacramento bridge, banishing Cal.P. across the river from the capital
city. Latham's hopes of a railroad empire tottered. He realized he
had no chance in a knock-down fight against opponents so opulent
on public bounty and asked for a conference with the Big Four with
the hope of "adjusting their problems." As well poke one's skull
inside a lion's jaws! The "adjustment" was completed by September
1st. The Central Pacific had complete control and Milton Latham
was out. There were now no independent railroads of any conse-
quence left in California.

Orientation map for Chapter VI showing proposed connection with the
Central Pacific, giving an 83¾ mile route to Sacramento.

VI

Brief Interlude with the Big Four

THE PEOPLE of Sonoma County did not view with joy the fact that their railway was now also part of the Central Pacific system. As they feared, rates were upped immediately. Construction came to a halt between Sonoma and Adelante, and on the long promised Bloomfield branch which Latham had finally started. They were afraid the road would never get beyond Healdsburg; but in November a contract was let to Turton & Knox for the seventeen miles to Cloverdale, and some activity was resumed toward Bloomfield.

Leland Stanford and his three partners were actually a bit undecided about the S.F. & N.P. They were still up in the air about their western terminal. They were using Oakland, and had been making plays for "Goat" Island and large tracts of San Francisco waterfront. Now they considered Saucelito very seriously. A surveyed line from there to Sacramento measured only eighty-three and three-fourths miles and required no ferry across Carquinez Straits. The little brick monument erected by the C.P. surveyors in front of Green's Hotel near the water's edge in Saucelito became almost a town shrine as the few score citizens gazed at it wonderingly and visualized their hamlet becoming the Jersey City of the West.

While the fate of its southern end remained the subject of conjecture, the Central Pacific quartette lost no time in extending the Petaluma and Humboldt Division northward to qualify for the entire Sonoma County subsidy before the deadline of June 21, 1872. The

Howe truss bridge across the Russian River was ready for rails by Christmas, and engineer George Black had 250 men toiling on the roadbed. A hard winter made the time remaining look very short, but Central Pacific speed and experience put rails into Cloverdale by the middle of March. The Bloomfield Branch, however, was formally abandoned. Stanford said it was too late to build it in time for the subsidy, and it wouldn't pay without it. An election down in Marin County subsidizing a new road, the North Pacific Coast, about which much more later, very likely had a large effect on their decision.

On Friday, March 15th, the opening passenger train ran through to Cloverdale. J. G. Dow of Healdsburg was aboard, first white man to blaze the route back in the spring of '49. The old man and his fellow passengers found a booming town nestling in the mountains at the head of Russian River Valley. The residents of Cloverdale expected their town to be the railroad's northern terminal for many years to come. All the trade of Mendocino, Lake, and upper Sonoma counties would reach its railroad here. A toll road to the Geysers was almost finished. Tourists would stage over it to view the "Devil's Gristmill" and the "Witches' Cauldron"; they would put up at Mr. Genkhart's United States Hotel or Mr. Simpson's hostelry, The Cloverdale, when they returned; and new lots were being laid out to tempt them to stay and make their homes there.

A few weeks later the road suffered a unique and stupid accident. Some of the railroaders got up a little housewarming ball in the new Geyserville depot. Two or three of them pumped a handcar up the line to call for some particularly comely farmers' daughters. As usual, the girls weren't ready and the boys had to wait, but finally the whole party was clinging to the little car, speeding through the night to the dance. Out in front with legs dangling sat two of the prettiest girls; behind them the boys put all they had into the armstrong mechanism. The delay, however, had stirred curiosity at Geyserville, and another handcar was speeding north with an investigating party. The two small cars collided at full speed in utter darkness. The girls in front had their legs broken and one of them died. All on both cars were badly injured. This ended unofficial festivities on railroad property.

In June a new San Francisco & North Pacific Railroad Company, capitalized at $12,350,000 was incorporated by the Big Four. Its intention, the articles stated, was to complete the road from San Francisco, via Saucelito, to Humboldt Bay with a connection from San Rafael to their main line near Vallejo. A ten million dollar bond issue was floated in New York. It looked as if the aspirations of Saucelito might be realized.

But with the new year, 1873, came an announcement that startled all. The Central Pacific had sold the San Francisco & North Pacific back to Peter Donahue! It was a step completely contrary to C.P. determination to monopolize California's transportation. But, it appeared, of the Big Four only Governor Stanford had taken much interest in the line. The others inclined toward Ralston's views of its territory as "coyote range" and felt it could play no part in their plans. As for Donahue, the Los Angeles electorate two months before had chosen S. P. in preference to the Texas & Pacific project to their city, in which he would have had an important part. There is room for endless speculation on possible connections between the two developments.

Peter Donahue had sold his road two years ago for $750,000. Now he bought it back with its seventeen-mile Cloverdale extension for an even million. But before we investigate what he did with it now, let us look at the North Pacific Coast Railroad, hitherto only briefly mentioned.

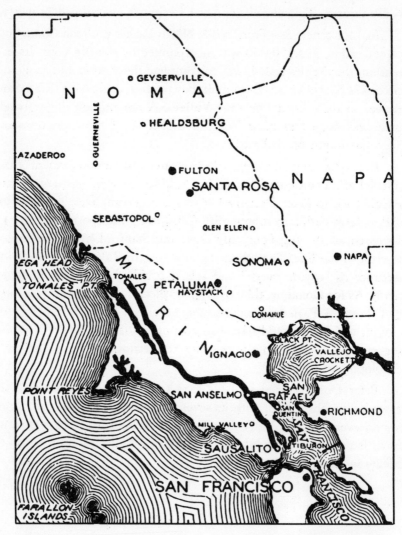

Orientation map for Chapter VII showing the Narrow Gauge with both
the Sausalito and San Quentin steamer connections.

VII

The Narrow Gauge Gets Started

THE REDWOOD timber conveniently adjacent to San Francisco was pretty completely logged off by the close of the sixties. Stands more remote began to come into the picture. One of the choicest of these grew in three gulches tributary to the western Russian River and owned chiefly by Austin D. Moore, Charles Howard of the Spring Valley Water Company, and W. H. Tillinghast under the name of Russian River Land and Lumber Company. They had wisely maintained this forest in its virgin state, but now began to plan for active lumbering.

Transportation from this remote area would be the problem. True, it was close to the ocean, but the treacherous, fog-bound and storm-swept coast with its complete lack of good harbors did not encourage dependence on the sea. During the winter of 1871-72 more than a quarter of the entire coastwise fleet was wrecked and the steam schooner, later used in the "dog-hole" redwood ports of the Mendocino coast, had not yet been developed. The narrow gauge railroad, however, was the latest development of science and appeared to be the answer.

Moore wanted to build the railroad from Saucelito to San Rafael, north across the ridge called the *puerto suello,* and then run northwesterly through more or less open country to the timberlands. But Howard and some of the other lumber company directors also owned large tracts around Point Reyes and prevailed on him to give up this

41

easy route in favor of a line that would serve the Point Reyes district
too. Among these persuasive friends was Warren Dutton, a '49 gold
hunter from Indiana, who, since 1852, had been digging tubers at
Tomales instead of nuggets. Indeed, he had pioneered potato culture
in northern California and, with a smart young farm hand named
Luther Burbank, materially improved the crop. Now he was shipping
many thousand tons of "Bodega Spuds" yearly from the little port
at Ocean Roar.

This more westerly route resulted in a most picturesque location,
but one which would be most expensive to build and operate. There
was, however, some justification for running a railroad on the coast
side. Twenty-five miles north of Saucelito a rich pocket of redwood
timber on Paper Mill Creek would be tapped. Taylor's paper mill
itself and the powder mill close by would be traffic sources. A well
developed dairy industry between Olema and Valley Ford shipped
two million pounds of butter to the city every year in "fast freight"
wagons that were, however, too slow to handle milk before it soured.
There were grain fields and ranches running sheep, hogs and cattle.
And, of course, potatoes.

The Articles of Incorporation of the North Pacific Coast Railroad
Company of California were filed December 16, 1871; capital stock
of a million and a half. Moore wanted a county subsidy of $160,000.
It was more than the new 5 per cent Railroad Law authorized, but
the Legislature granted special exemption and Marin went to the
polls on January 29th and authorized the gift. Dutton's village of
Tomales, its 200 residents making it second largest in the county,
approved 12-1. A railroad sounded heavenly here — there wasn't
even a wagon road to San Rafael except around by Petaluma, and
that a sorry dirt affair with a succession of gates to open. Saucelito
did not record an adverse vote. But Bolinas, whose boatmen carried
produce to market in their little sloops, was 20-1 against. Over all,
the measure carried by better than 2-1.

The county supervisors accordingly resolved to award the subsidy
to the North Pacific Coast and Austin Moore proceeded at once with

the detailed survey of the route to which he had become committed. Between San Rafael and the head of Tomales Bay loomed White's Hill. Well he knew that it would be no picnic to surmount, but Gus Cox, his engineer, found the terrain even worse than expected. Moreover, Cox reported, the fifteen-mile stretch along the shore of Tomales Bay would require almost continuous trestle, costly to build, maintain and protect from fire.

Whereupon the newborn company practically ground to a standstill. The route was definitely specified in the subsidy contract — Saucelito to San Rafael and over White's Hill to Tomales — to alter it was to forfeit $160,000. Moore, vexed at having been talked out of his original plans, attempted to resume them. He made a counterproposal to the county: the N. P. C. would renounce the subsidy just approved provided a new gift of $325,000 was voted; with this assistance it would build two railroads — a main line Saucelito to San Rafael, across the *puerto suello* to Novato, along San Antonio Creek to Tomales and thence northward, and, later, a branch from San Rafael to the redwoods of Paper Mill Creek.

As a demonstration of good faith, construction was started at White's Hill, July 25th. A note in the *Marin County Journal* that two wheelbarrows were sent to the job reflects the scale of operations. But the supervisors turned down this new plan cold. Marin County was becoming skeptical of the North Pacific Coast Railroad Company. To make matters worse, the surveyors now found the ridge directly south of San Rafael a matter of costly construction—$70,000 could be saved by running the road through Ross Valley a few miles west with a side track to San Rafael. Moore's bankers insisted on the cheaper route, and again he had to ask the supervisors to authorize a change.

The Rafaelites were up in arms. They had an aggressive leader, William Tell Coleman, who had just invested heavily in San Rafael real estate. Coleman was a Kentuckian who had come to California to dig gold but gone into business instead. When gangs of "hoodlums" terrorized San Francisco in the Fifties he became president of the Vigilante Committee that cleaned them out and gave the city a graft-free municipal government. He could have won any political office in the State and was even boomed for President, but sternly refused all invitations to run. The Rafaelites demanded that Moore stick by his original commitments. They told him what he was pretty sure of anyway — that if he hadn't promised to run his main line through the county seat where a third of all the voters lived, his subsidy wouldn't have had a chance.

The petition was argued at a jammed open meeting of the three-man Board of Supervisors, February 6, 1873. Moore and Dutton presented the railroad's case while Coleman and others spoke at great length and some heat in opposition. They recessed for supper and then talked some more. It was not until eleven o'clock that the Supervisors finally voted — two to one to allow the change. San Rafael was to be left out on a sidetrack!

Now, at least, the North Pacific Coast Railroad was ready to go ahead. Moore arranged with the Saucelito Land & Ferry Company for terminal facilities and a right-of-way through its property, being required by the Big Four to stipulate that no interference with any plans of the Central Pacific would result. The Railroad House and the Grand Hotel added extra rooms to accommodate the workmen. Chinamen by the wagon load with their tools and tents rolled through the streets of San Rafael, all bound for White's Hill. Another crew started operations near Ross Landing. By the end of February, 600 men were gandy-dancing on the narrow gauge.

The work had been going on for a couple of months when Austin Moore was suddenly struck with a staggering realization. There had been no formal ceremony of breaking ground! This would never do. So on April 10th, he staged the necessary rites before a ferry load of friends and bigwigs at Saucelito. Solemnly, he shoveled a little dirt around and a gang knocked together a few hundred feet of track. Then the party enjoyed a free meal and listened to Moore's predictions for his railway. His trains, he told them, would run to San Rafael by the Fourth of July; to Russian River in another year, then to the contemplated temporary terminus, Walhalla (now spelled Gualala). Later the narrow gauge would build on through Humboldt County — maybe clear to the Columbia River. Coleman, unimpressed, brought suit in Federal Court to abrogate the subsidy because of the change in route and to force the N. P. C. to pay $50,000 damages to San Rafael in addition.

By September the usually tranquil hills swarmed with 1300 Chinamen, queues swinging like pendulums under black silk skullcaps or wide straw hats as they wielded picks and shovels. Usually quiet and industrious, quite a fracas had ensued at Paper Mill Creek when Ah Sin, their paymaster, decamped with the payroll and they decided to hang his brother for the crime. But thirty miles of grade was finished. Tunnel No. 1, a short one, was ready for the rails. Chief Engineer Howard Schuyler, recently secured from the D. & R. G., reported that the main White's Hill tunnel was in about 500 feet with three eight-hour shifts pounding away in each heading. No. 3 was about to be holed in and No. 4, under Warren Dutton's property near Tomales, had been subcontracted by that gentleman himself. Richardson's Bay echoed to the "sisss-bum! sisss-bum!" of the Pacific Bridge Company's pile drivers and anguished howls of protest from oyster growers who claimed their prize bivalves were so unstrung that they refused to propagate. At Saucelito the wharf was finished and a mile and a half of thirty-five pound rail spiked down as far as the roundhouse and shops, themselves near completion. Two locomotives and a score of flat cars were on the way.

Hopes of operation during 1873 were given up, however. Announcing that winter time construction was impractical, Moore closed down the job in October. His real reason was lack of funds—already $600,000 had been spent — and he left for Europe to seek additional financing.

Work on the big 1,250-foot tunnel was continued, however, and in March, J. H. Bugbee, the contractor, staged a "holing through" party. There were about fifty in the group — directors, county supervisors, etc., shepherded by Howard Schuyler. At noon, he marshalled them near the west portal and advised them to cover their ears. Thirty-two blasts of giant powder exploding simultaneously proved his suggestion sound. Then with candles dimly gleaming in the smoke they ventured inside to find the job well done. A six-foot hole had been blasted into the other heading and the center lines jibed within a quarter inch.

Outside again, in Bugbee's shack, champagne was ready iced. The safe return of Austin Moore with enough money to finish the railroad was very earnestly toasted. Schuyler raised his glass to the "Greatest Bore in Marin County" but one of the N. P. C. directors filed an exception before the toast was drunk. He named no names but William Tell Coleman and his lawsuit was in every mind.

President Moore did return with funds — not as ample as he had hoped, but enough to resume the work. Again prairie schooners loaded down with Chinese, their picks and shovels, and their rice and tea, rolled in long trains through San Rafael, while several hundred of their fellow Celestials clambered ashore from a little steamer at Ocean Roar to start working south.

Locomotive No. 1, the "Saucelito," had been unloaded on Oakland wharf back in December while the job was shut down. Now, on the 15th day of June, 1874, the graceful little twenty-ton Baldwin 4-4-0 finally floated over to her namesake town and was installed on N. P. C. rails. Soon pungent wood smoke poured from her balloon stack and she was hauling a construction train. Two more engines were on the way, and the Kimball factory in San Francisco was about to ship five passenger coaches. Carter Brothers had a contract for some cars as well; they were setting up a shop in Saucelito, and here they would remain until they opened their big factory in Newark three years later.

Iron went down rapidly. The narrow gauge track stretched about a mile a day. It reached the spot where surveyors' stakes marked the turnout for the "sidetrack" to San Rafael, a region uninhabited except for Louis Canopa's Mountain Top House on the crest of a little

N.P.C. No. 9 M. S. LATHAM ran into a bull on the way to San Quentin on April 17, 1882.

Making more steam. A double-header stalled on White's Hill.

One of the first trains into Mill Valley, 1889.

North Pacific Coast engine No. 6 VALLEY FORD.

Robert H. Menzies

red hill close by. The railroad builders named the place "The Junction." It is now San Anselmo.

To soothe the Rafaelites, Schuyler now concentrated on the "branch." Moore said he'd have a train in the county seat by the 25th of July and gave the order to work nights and Sundays. As the sweating Chinamen approached, the local folks tramped out on the dusty right-of-way to watch them, but were able to clean up later in their new Universal Baths, the latest gadget fad. The less conservative physicians were beginning to favor occasional bathing, and, as few homes boasted bathrooms, this popular contraption of white rubber and wooden frame, suspended between two chairs and adjustable by drawstring to fit adult or infant, was being peddled very successfully around the county.

The rails passed the town limit posts on the very day that Moore had fixed, and the "Saucelito" steamed in with a string of flats, announcing her arrival with a volley of whistle blasts. Over on B Street, Engineer Bonney in the "San Rafael's" cab replied. As the *Journal* put it:

> "While the engine was at this end of the line, its whistle shrieking and screaming at its utmost, so all the people might hear, the locomotive on the San Rafael and San Quentin Railroad hearing, set up an answering blow and the two machines gave a regular engine chorus for some time which attracted much attention. First the low deep notes which hint of suppressed power — then the other would reply in a loud shrieking whistle suggestive of brag and bluster, then the short, sharp notes of defiance and competition, only to be followed by the more prolonged and full-throated strains of fraternal welcome and congratulation. Then the hills took up the echoes and spoke them to the sea and the chorus of the engines was ended."

A week later the track was laid to B Street and Director Tillinghast brought in a hundred guests on a train of flat cars. Most of them were Army folk, including the crack Presidio Band, and they took over the vacant Tamalpais Hotel for lunch and dancing. Again the *Journal:* "(it was) the pioneer picnic over our little road, but who shall number those to follow?" Prophetic words! But they were not all to be so dignified.

September first found the N. P. C. still with only one locomotive but with its rails through tunnel No. 1 and nearing the big White's Hill bore. It was now in heavy, expensive country. Just between the two tunnels were six trestles, and almost continuous winding deep cut and fill marked the whole section. Down in the valley, one farmer Dickson could sit on his front porch and watch through the laurels as the engine almost completely circled his house. It gained eighty-three feet of altitude in the process, but it took three miles of track to advance a mile. Building it had been a nasty job—hauling 10 x 12 bridge timbers, seventy feet long across the canyons and up steep, manzanita clad hillsides.

Another locomotive finally arrived to help out, named "Olema." Of the same size and weight as the "Saucelito," she had a third greater flue heating surface and was a much better steamer. The older loco-motive was loaded on a barge with a few flats and shipped to To-males. The whole population trooped over to Ocean Roar to see her landed, while resident Director Warren Dutton shouted orders to the sailors and roustabouts.

With construction trains operating on both ends, the tempo of the job increased. Dutton announced that he would celebrate the opening with a barbecue the likes of which had rarely been seen. Early storms granted a few extra weeks of life to numerous pigs, oxen, and turkeys, but on Thursday, January 7, 1875, these jointly exuded delectable aromas as they browned before charcoal fires. In the immense new railroad warehouse, built by the resident director, its floor at car deck height over sunken tracks, the good housewives of Tomales gaily spread their best linens; arrayed their home-made pies, their thick iced cakes, their biscuits and their piccalilli.

It was dark and foggy in San Francisco when Austin Moore, his fellow N. P. C. officials and 300 guests boarded the *Petaluma of Saucelito* at Davis Street Wharf. But on the Marin side, the sun pushed through the rising mist to glint on the burnished "Saucelito" and "Olema," steaming together at the head end of eight lemon-colored coaches. Soon the first train sped gaily along the shore at the foot of the wooded hills, across the long trestle to Strawberry Point, over Collins summit, and through Corte Madera to The Junction. It backed over to San Rafael to add that city's delegation, then on again for Tomales.

Everywhere the train met welcome. Flags flapped all along the line and everybody was out to wave and cheer. The guests, to most of whom the country was entirely new, stared out the windows in growing amazement as the pull up White's Hill started; at the rugged rural beauty and the heavy railroading required to conquer it. James Fowler, Valley Ford pioneer, whipped an envelope out of his pocket and dashed off:

> It twisted in and twisted out
> And left the traveller still in doubt
> Whether the snake that made the track
> Was going up or coming back.

Then down grade, the new-fangled air brakes operating smoothly and through the redwoods along Paper Mill Creek, and finally for miles on the shore of shallow Tomales Bay. Nicasio, Olema (fondly known as Bulltown), Marshalls, sounded their notes of welcome, but Tomales outdid them all. As the train approached, the visitors could see the hilltops lined with shouting villagers and the building festooned with bunting. Warren Dutton bade them welcome in the name of the railroad, the county, and the town, and opened the door of his warehouse bulging with gastronomic delights.

The food gone and all belts loosened, the resident director beckoned them to gather around a little platform at the end of the building for a few speeches. Moore expressed his general satisfaction with the events to date and said the N. P. C. would proceed at once on up the coast. Then he made a startling announcement: Milton S. Latham had acquired 60 per cent of the capital stock! The ex-Cal.P. operator was back in the railroad business.

Judge Shafter told the crowd that more money had gone into the North Pacific Coast than any other road west of the Rockies, Central

Pacific included. He was referring to stockholders' money and thus probably was quite accurate. Warren Dutton explained:

"First we thought we could get English or foreign cheap money. After spending a certain amount a crisis came on, and we could not get the money to build it as all other roads are built (subsidies). What was to be done? Who would take California money out of the vaults and build it? Mr. Moore stuck to it, and succeeded in drawing the attention of capitalists to it. The stockholders were called on to double up, and the most of us did it. But we finally enlisted a man who cares more to build up public enterprises than any other man in the state. He looked at it, concluded it would pay, and put in his money. Capitalists generally ask, What security can you give? What interest will it pay? But we found a man with a brain grand enough to see the merit of this work, and a heart, big enough to aid it, and we should give him all praise."

They gave him three cheers. He was not present to acknowledge them. They gave Dutton three cheers and a tiger and three cheers with no tiger for Moore. The ladies of Tomales were accorded a triple hurrah and then there was another set for Latham, from whom, they began to realize, all blessings would henceforth flow. Then the excursionists climbed aboard their double-header and Tomales had had its big day.

Appropriately enough, the first freight shipped was 3,000 sacks of potatoes. Regular passenger service started January 11th with about a hundred on the train. The Pacific Steamship Company pulled the *Monterey* off the Tomales run and the stage line to Petaluma folded. "Duttonville" was on the railroad, the train left daily at 8 a.m. Three times a week there was a mixed train in the afternoon as well and Sundays would see excursions. The town boomed, and there was an epidemic of moving houses to get closer to the tracks. Old fogies wrote: "we have lived in a semi-stupor so long . . . that to be stirred up so suddenly by the shrill whistle of the great equalizer and civilizer leaves us in a condition of bewilderment." And rancher, general store proprietor, Congressman, contractor, ship operator, resident-director Warren Dutton added to these titles that of station agent.

The shrill whistle of the great equalizer was snuffed out after one week by storm and washouts and heard no more for a month. Open again, the road still had its troubles. The unsettled roadbed was rough and derailments monotonously frequent. Tunnels suffered cave-ins and drenched passengers had to circumnavigate them through the mud. Those contemplating trips via narrow gauge were advised in the press to go well prepared with food:

". . . it is a journey full of stops and some of the people along the road would skin a flea for its hide. You commence to believe you have journeyed and fallen among thieves. One bereaved widow who hasn't nine small children at the breast, sells bread at 50¢ a slice and then tries to make believe she is conferring a favor.

An Olema man wrote:

Articles extolling the North Pacific Coast Railroad are all humbug . . . It may be pleasant to hear the whistle, but try a trip on the train. When playfully inclined, the engine practices Olympic sports such as jumping off the track, etc., etc., the rear car bumping along over the ties on the trestle instead of the rails and other incidental frolics peculiar to the narrow gauge."

That all this was not just idle griping was proved in April when a strong gale blew the rear coach of a southbound train clear off the track. It rolled down the forty-foot fill and landed upside down in a duck farm, only the seats within saving the passengers from being squashed between roof and floor. President Moore rushed to the wreck and personally directed the rescue work. Luckily none were dead, but many were painfully injured. A few days before an engine had flopped off the rails and landed, wheels up, in Tomales Bay. Grim forerunners of things to come.

For months the North Pacific Coast management had dickered with the San Rafael and San Quentin about a merger. Affectionately known as the "Bobtail Railroad," the latter still shuttled back and forth and, with the late Charlie Minturn's old *Contra Costa* (now refurbished and improved with a copper bottom and seventeen-bucket wheels), it provided a leisurely ride to San Francisco. When the "San Rafael" was laid up for repairs and the "dummy" hauled the pumpkin colored cars, the ride was leisurely indeed.

The Rafaelites fondly believed that, given frequent, cheap transportation, the entire east bay population would pack up and emigrate over to their elysian climate. For example:

"Berkeley [proclaimed the *Tocsin*] is a Godforsaken plain, scourged by wind, brooded over by fog, treeless with only a background of desolate squirrel-cursed hills to relieve the universal gloom. The climate is by no means conducive to general health, having in it the seeds of malaria, miasma, general shakes and various other ills that flesh is heir to. Nevertheless, people live there . . . instead of coming to San Rafael . . . because commutation tickets can be bought for $3 a month."

Perhaps, they thought, the narrow gauge would provide such good service that Berkeley would be abandoned to the squirrels. They favored a merger. From the N. P. C. point of view, acquisition of the older line would eliminate competition between San Rafael and the City; it would reduce operating costs by substituting the short, level haul from San Quentin to San Anselmo for the long pull from Saucelito over Collins Summit (though it was a bit late to think about that); and it would cinch the subsidy, still held up by Coleman's suit, with a main line through San Rafael.

But the old Vigilante wanted no truck with the North Pacific Coast. He tried to take over the S. R. & S. Q. himself, promising more trips, lower fares, and permanent freedom from any unholy alliance with the narrow gauge. The stockholders, all his fellow townsmen, gave him a chance to buy the little road, but Latham had the inside track with the ferry company. In March, 1875, Adolf Mailliard signed the lease of the Bobtail Railroad to the N. P. C., which, by its terms, agreed to run at least three round trips daily through San Quentin and to cut the fare to the City to half a dollar.

The "San Rafael" hauled her last train down to the Point on the 29th; then, loaded on a narrow gauge flat, went to Saucelito to be scrapped. Next day, all the commuters rode over Collins Summit while the gandy dancers pried up one rail of the S.R. & S.Q. and spiked it down again 1 foot 8½ inches closer to its mate. And on April 1st they rode on red plush seats in the light yellow N. P. C.

coaches instead of the familiar slat benches of the orange Bobtail cars to the San Quentin ferry.

The narrow gauge made the new route its main passenger artery. The Saucelito-Strawberry Point-Corte Madera route saw freights only and one "horse-shoe" commuter train. With the cheaper, more frequent service, travel skyrocketed. The San Quentin train usually carried four well-filled coaches. Now running time to the city was the same as from Broadway, Oakland. But few Berkeleyites moved to marvelous Marin.

Orientation map for Chapter VIII showing extension of the Sonoma
& Marin Railway Co. from the old Petaluma & Haystack.

VIII

A Railroad for the Gophers

IN THE MEANTIME, the Rafaelites, led by Coleman and aided by Petaluma, had been trying for two years to acquire still another railroad. When Peter Donahue again took over the San Francisco & North Pacific in January of '73, he planned to extend not only northward but also south to the Bay. The ferry ride to Donahue was tedious, and the Colonel had thought of building down to San Rafael, leasing trackage rights and laying a broad gauge rail on the N. P. C. to Saucelito or, perhaps, acquiring the Bobtail Line himself. On surveying the terrain he found it was not as simple as he had expected. A 1,200-foot tunnel through the *puerto suello* behind the county seat and a long bridge across the creek at Donahue would by themselves cost a quarter of a million, and the Colonel had already extended himself pretty far in buying back the road.

So he made a proposition to the people of San Rafael at a mass meeting Coleman arranged in the new Court House. If they would take care of the bridge and the tunnel, he would do the rest. He did not want a subsidy, and Coleman was heard to say that was good, folks were a bit sore on subsidies. Cash he did not ask, either; he had "credit at a hardware store" and could start to build the road any time. What he would like were pledges of gold coin, to be payable when the first passenger train ran from Donahue to Point San Quentin. But this time the genial Colonel's eloquence laid an egg. Though Judge Pixley warned them Marin County would never amount to shucks unless they gave up their old fogey dislike of being in debt, the Rafaelites kept their hands in their pockets.

Donahue thus bowing out for the time, Coleman, who had had some railroad experience back in Illinois before the Gold Rush, and banker I. G. Wickersham of Petaluma undertook to organize a company. One October afternoon in 1874, a large fleet of buggies and buckboards were parked around Johnson's General Store in Novato. In them had arrived most of the wealth, brains, and gumption in the two counties. Also present was one Joseph Kohn with a working model of his Crew Prismoidal Railway and large hopes of selling it to the assembled leading citizens.

Wisely tabling an invitation to visit a local vineyard until after their business powwow, they listened to Coleman expound on the need for quick transit and low fares from Petaluma south. They had expected the Central Pacific to provide this service, he told them, then Donahue, but both had failed them and it was folly to wait any longer. Besides, such a road would pay big dividends. As he put it:

> "Donahue's railroad pays $1,000 a day, yet it is all inland; it stops up a creek, runs up into the country, and has no deep water landing. The little San Rafael road pays $30,000 a year, yet it has worked under great disadvantage. It pays interest on a $40,444 mortgage, and while it is but three miles long, it has nearly all the expenses of a 40-mile road. (!) If this little road, with its limited travel, can build and repair and run and make $30,000 a year and Donahue's road can make $1,000 a day, I ask you how much a road from San Francisco to Petaluma, through this magnificent county could pay?"

There was only one way to find out, so they organized the Sonoma & Marin Railway Company on the spot. A few days later the same group met again in the Petaluma Theater, argued a while about the relative merits of standard gauge, narrow gauge and the Crew Prismoidal System and decided to go first class. Capital stock was fixed at one million dollars. I. G. Wickersham, a Petaluman since 1852 and head of the First National Gold Bank, was chosen president, but Coleman, now a large scale subdivider in San Rafael, was vice-president and continued to be the actual mainspring of the enterprise. The terminal cities were each asked to raise $200,000 and Novato half of that amount. The McNears offered an acre of land to all Petalumans who took five shares of stock.

Possibly this inducement explains why Petaluma's quota was soon subscribed while the other towns lagged behind. The surveyors were instructed not only to map the line as planned, but also to run a line to San Pedro Point, a McNear owned promontory north of San Rafael, just in case the latter fell down.

On March 23, 1875, the S. & M. purchased the old Petaluma & Haystack Railroad — still carrying the mail along its rickety track by oat power. A month later the survey was complete. From the old Minturn Line depot in Petaluma to a junction with the North Pacific Coast in San Rafael was just twenty-two miles, all but five of which were in Marin.

All this activity stirred Milton Latham's fertile imagination, and he sent Dutton over to Petaluma to make a deal with Wickersham. The N. P. C. would lease the new road (if the S. & M. would build it narrow gauge) and would promise to run two passenger trains and a freight daily. It would pay, as annual rent, 8 per cent of cost of construction and after two years would buy the road at cost if the stockholders wished to sell. Or, as an alternative, the North Pacific Coast would just provide rolling stock for the S. & M. at certain specified rentals. The Petaluma banker said thanks very much — he'd think it over.

Midyear saw grading and tunnel contracts awarded. Ground was broken at Rudesill's Landing (where the P. & H. ended), on July 2nd, and both jobs got under way. In a couple of months the grade from Haystack to Novato was almost finished and then things started to go wrong. The stockholders were slow with their assessments. Both the tunnel and grading contractors failed. But the main difficulty was that there was really no railroad organization. None of the officers drew a salary; they regarded it as a civic project meriting part of their spare time. The Petaluma *Argus* wailed:

"The North Pacific Coast Railroad is 54 miles of rail across bays, through mountains, over hills, spanning streams, jumping chasms, in fact encountering and overcoming every obstacle that ever impeded a railroad to reach — Tomales! Petaluma wants 21 miles of road through a level country to reach San Francisco, and with all our capitalists, it will be as much as ever if she accomplishes it. Tomales is a town of 200 inhabitants — Petaluma is a city of nearly 5,000. The destinies of Tomales are directed by one man (Warren Dutton) — those of Petaluma are confounded by the clamor of many. Oh, for a Napoleon to lead us to victory!"

William Tell Coleman was probably as near a Napoleon as the West had then to offer, but he and Wickersham, under the press of other affairs, probably rued ever starting the S. & M. They tried again to make a deal with Donahue, but his best offer was to accept the property as a gift and finish it if and when convenient. Wearily they readvertised for bids and let new contracts. Again the booming of black powder in the *puerto suello* was heard in San Rafael.

A year passed and the job was still poking along. Only ten miles of roadbed through the marshes south of Petaluma and a mile from San Rafael to the tunnel were ready for iron, and there was no iron. There was no rolling stock either, except for Minturn's battered relics. The tunnel heading, 80 feet in, had 1,120 feet yet to go. Only $60,000 in actual cash had been collected — it had all gone into this construction. The growing business depression made prospects bleak, while the anti-Chinese riots which it bred in San Francisco had old Vigilante Coleman raring to collect a posse and giving little thought to the railroad.

Obviously the Sonoma & Marin Railway was never going to turn a wheel unless there was some drastic change in the way its affairs were going. The directors' meeting on October '76 forced the issue. A few wanted to decide on a gauge (even this had not been settled), buy some rails, and keep on plugging. But most of them, including Coleman and Wickersham, wanted to get out from under on any terms. None were railroaders nor had they any real wish to be. They lined up a committee to dicker with both the North Pacific Coast and the San Francisco & North Pacific and decided to take the best deal offered.

Petaluma and San Rafael awaited the outcome anxiously. Each had developed an aversion for the railroad that already served it and prayed the other would acquire the S. & M. Latham, in the East buying ferryboats for his narrow gauge, wired he wasn't interested. But Peter Donahue was. He paid the $85,000 that had been expended, took over stock, franchise and roadbed, and agreed to have trains running by May. The poultry city mourned the victory of the man who made it a way station on the road to Donahue, but the Rafaelites rejoiced. "Had the managers of the narrow gauge secured the road, our thriving town would continue to be the abused slave to a tyrant monopoly" was the way the *Herald* put it. With Colonel Donahue it could look for lower fares, better service, and, most likely, a San Quentin terminal where ships would load local products for such ports as Le Havre and Liverpool. In fact, the editor opined, San Rafael would probably be the *"entrepot* of the grand truck lines from New York, Baltimore, St. Louis and Chicago" and make Vallejo look sick.

The Donahue staff took over and the tempo of construction became full throttle. The woodpecker pace in the *puerto suello* tunnel gave way to around-the-clock shifts and daylight holed through in February. The Colonel's old war horse engine "San Jose," was moved over to the P. & H. with a string of flats to be the construction train. An old ferryboat was moored in the creek for a boarding house and 200 Chinamen hired. Using Orientals was unusual for the S. F. & N. P. proprietor; probably the Irish were all busy swinging shillelahs in the San Francisco riots. Coleman was busy there too, back in vigilante harness. He had armed a "committee" with 6,000 hickory pick-handles and saved the city from mobs determined to burn it to the ground, a feat that might later have elected him President of the United States, had he not refused to run.

September of '77 saw the rails from the north enter San Rafael. It seemed that a few more weeks would finish the job although

Donahue appeared undecided where to cross Petaluma Creek to connect with his S. F. & N. P. But more months passed and still no trains ran on the Sonoma & Marin. The last bits of construction dragged interminably. It almost looked as if the Colonel was loathe to see his namesake town lose its importance as a terminal and was stalling. Not until August 31, 1878, did an impromptu excursion train make the first run from Petaluma to San Rafael. It was followed, on September 19th, by an official grand opening excursion from Cloverdale and way points. Some 2,000 junketeers and a couple of brass bands arrived in two trains over the S. F. & N. P. and the Sonoma & Marin. They picnicked at Magnolia Park where the San Rafael housewives had spread so large an array of delectables that extensive leftovers were next day divided between St. Vincent's Orphanage and the poor. Chief Fecunto, the Digger Indian Emperor Norton of San Rafael, "collected taxes" in full military regalia and a plumed shako until thrown into the calaboose to sober up.

Coleman delivered the address of welcome. Peter Donahue was not among those present. Apparently he still regarded the S. & M. as a step-child.

The following week was that of the Sonoma and Marin Fair at Petaluma, and the Sonoma & Marin ran a daily train for a $2.00 round trip fare. But then all operations ceased! There was no explanation—there were no trains either. Throughout the entire Fall the almost virgin rails grew rusty. In January the Petaluma *Courier* reported:

> ". . . the gophers have taken possession of the . . . railroad and are rooting out the ties and rails. Go-pher them, little fellows as they are of no practical use, the sooner they are thrown out of the way the better.
>
> Yes [agreed the San Rafael *Herald*] but the gophers are out of a job, for the recent rain swept the entire road away, leaving only the hole in the tunnel."

Two months later the continued storms caused even the tunnels to cave in.

When summer came Donahue fixed up the track again and ran one train daily for a while. The route grew popular and travelers to and from Mendocino, Lake and Sonoma Counties began to favor it, changing cars to the narrow gauge at San Rafael. The *James M. Donahue,* crack steamer of the S. F. & N. P., plied up the creek with fewer and fewer passengers, and the Colonel didn't like it. In September he announced that all service on the S. & M. was abolished. On popular entreaty he delayed the move while the 1879 Sonoma and Marin Fair was on, but he juggled the schedule to miss connections with the N. P. C. and force any passengers to stop overnight in San Rafael. Then the S. & M. was again left to the gophers.

Never had the good citizens of Sonoma and Marin dreamed of such a contretemps. Coleman, Wickersham, and the other S. & M. promoters were particularly irate. They had a bill introduced in Sacramento which made failure to operate a railway for six months mean confiscation of the owner's rights and reversion of right-of-way. With chances good that this measure would become law, and the return of summer, the Colonel again restored the daily train on the Sonoma & Marin. But there was still no station, no office, no agent and no published timetable. Connections with the N. P. C. were sketchy at best. If the Petaluma train was late, passengers would find the narrow gauge had gone despite wires from the S. F. & N. P. to hold it; they would have to climb wearily back into the same cars, be hauled around to Donahue and land in the city along with the dawn. Nevertheless, wayfarers chose the route rather than endure the endless meanderings of Petaluma Creek.

The President of the United States did likewise. Visiting San Francisco, Rutherford B. Hayes received a bid to the Sonoma and Marin Fair. Hayes was a push-over for county fairs; he happily detoured hundreds of miles to take one in. Alighting from the narrow gauge in San Rafael to change cars for Petaluma, he lifted his silk hat and bowed to the crowd at the depot. However, no one recognized the Chief Executive. To them the silk topper indicated some one probably running a medicine show, and so they ignored him. Hayes, somewhat abashed, hastily boarded the broad gauge train.

Peter Donahue's coy dilly-dallying on the Sonoma & Marin Railway by no means extended to his operations of the San Francisco & North Pacific. Maintenance was excellent and ample schedules adhered to. He added two Grant built locomotives, "Cloverdale" and "Petaluma," to his four Union Iron Works engines and the "San Jose." Passenger and freight rolling stock was constantly improved and expanded.

For a while he considered proceeding with the long awaited Bloomfield branch, partly graded for years, rather than allow the N. P. C. to reach the district first, but gave it up. He considered, also, running a line down the Russian River to serve the various mills around Stumptown, or Guerneville as the camp, second only to Eureka in lumbering importance, had been rechristened. Their entire output was still hauled by ox team to the railroad.

Back in 1869, the stern-wheel steamer *Enterprise* had been put together at Heald's mill to carry lumber and passengers to the coast. Fifty feet long, she drew only a foot of water, and her skipper, Captain J. M. King, had hopes that in time of high water he could even ply upstream far enough to serve Healdsburg. A trial trip was all she made. The Russian River did not lend itself to navigation.

The mill owners offered Donahue free rights-of-way and bridge timbers if he'd build the branch but reneged after Antoine Korbel of the upstream mill had sold him on the deal. Donahue, disgusted, built only to Korbel's in May of '76, but a year later he went on to Guerneville.

Ken Kidder

A dignified gathering at Elim Grove just south of Cazadero on the N.P.C. circa 1886.

N.P.C. No. 6 VALLEY FORD with the commute train stops at "B" Street station, San Rafael in the '90s.

Ken Kidder

Sausalito terminal of the North Pacific Coast around the turn of the century.

N.P.C. No. 2, named SAN RAFAEL and nicknamed JACKRABBIT, with a picnic party at Mill Valley about 1890.

Construction of the second Mill Valley station, 1898. The old depot at far left.

N.P.C. No. 8 BULLY BOY leaving Sausalito with the Mill Valley train.

North Pacific Coast bridge across the Russian River at Duncan's Mills, 1891.

S. F. & N. P. RAILWAY
DONAHUE BROAD GAUGE

SUNDAY EXCURSIONS

GREAT REDUCTION IN RATES

STEAMER "TIBURON" LEAVES MARKET STREET WHARF AT

8.00 A. M. EVERY SUNDAY

AND CONNECTS WITH TRAIN AT
POINT TIBURON for SAN RAFAEL, SONOMA, GLEN ELLEN,
(Arrive in San Francisco, 6.05 P. M.)
PETALUMA, SANTA ROSA, HEALDSBURG, LITTON SPRINGS,
CLOVERDALE, GUERNEVILLE and WAY STATIONS. RE-
TURNING arrives in San Francisco, at 7.25 P. M.

EXCURSION TICKETS GOOD FOR

Sundays ✸ Only

AT THE FOLLOWING GREATLY REDUCED RATES

Petaluma and Return	......	$1.00	Sonoma and Return	....	$1.00
Santa Rosa	"	1.50	Verano	"	1.05
Fulton	"	1.75	Caliente	"	1.10
Healdsburg	"	2.25	Watriss	"	1.10
Litton Springs	"	2.40	Madrone	"	1.10
Cloverdale	"	3.00	Hills	"	1.15
Guerneville	"	2.50	Glen Ellen	"	1.20

TICKET OFFICE ᴬᵀ TIBURON FERRY

FOOT OF MARKET STREET

H. C. WHITING,
General Manager

PETER J. McGLYNN,
Gen. Pass. and Ticket Agent

S.F.& N.P.

S. F. & N. P. advertisement appearing in Bancroft's Railway Guide of
May, 1890.

Orientation map for Chapter IX showing location of the prismoidal railway. Solid line indicates portion built.

IX

The Leap Frog Line

PETER DONAHUE, the San Francisco & North Pacific proprietor, also had his eyes on some interesting developments over the hills to the east near the old town of Sonoma. Joseph S. Kohn, who had tried to interest the S. & M. promoters at Novato with his model prismoidal railway, was finally meeting with some success. He had plugged his curious system throughout California for years. He had almost won a San Francisco franchise for a line up Market Street and on to the Ocean Beach, but Ralston had persuaded the mayor to veto it. He had put on a demonstration in Los Angeles and sold the San Pedro Street Railroad, a five-mile line, only to see the deal similarly killed. He had been Johnny-on-the-spot at every railroad meeting in the state, and now at last he got a break.

The people of the old Mexican hamlet of Sonoma, where the Bear Flag was raised, had yearned for a railroad ever since the election of 1868 had awarded the main line to Petaluma. Yearning, however, had got them nowhere, and they still rode horseback to the steamer *Clinton* at the Embarcadero when they went down to the City — still saw ox teams haul their freight. When Kohn arranged a Sonoma railroad meeting in February of '75, he had found a willing audience.

The Crew Prismoidal System, he had told the Sonomans, was the safest and cheapest railway that money could buy. It was true that so far only one line was in operation — somewhere near Chicago — but it was the first of hundreds to follow. Mr. Crew of Opelika, Alabama, had invented it as a happy compromise between regular railroads and balloons. Engines and cars ran on a single rail laid atop a continuous wooden "prism" 30 inches wide at the base and 18 inches high. Auxiliary wheels preserved equilibrium by bearing on each side of the prism, but all weight and driving effort was exerted on the central rail. It was, summed up Joseph Kohn, positively the last word in railroading.

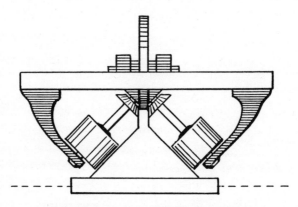

CROSS-SECTION OF RUNNING GEAR AND "PRISM"
from Sonoma Valley Prismoidal Ry. Prospectus

His listeners were convinced. They organized the Sonoma Valley Prismoidal Railway Company and, in June, 1876, actually commenced to build their hopeful experiment from Norfolk (near the Embarcadero) to the town. Much of the route was through tule marshes, and they had first to dump in fill for an earthen "prism" as a roadbed for their wooden one. In August the fabrication of this contraption was begun, and it devoured 68,000 feet of lumber for every mile. At Norfolk a steamer landing was built, also a large warehouse and car sheds. In San Francisco the Pacific Foundry was banging on a peg-leg locomotive.

On Thanksgiving Day the first section was ready for a public showing. Just by chance, the three and a half mile track through the tules ended in a large field Joe Kohn had bought and was laying out for a town. As guests of that promoter, a goodly assemblage of notables came up on the *Sonoma* and walked ashore where she tied up at the new Norfolk wharf. It was a bright sunshiny morning. The first train of the Sonoma Valley Prismoidal Railway steamed in waiting — a curious locomotive whose two drivers rested on the rounded top rail that crowned the prism like a bicycle on a tight rope, but sustained from toppling by inclined rollers bearing on the wooden prism faces. A small boiler delivered steam to the two cylinder engine connected directly to the drivers and a crankhead eccentric operated a link motion for reversing.

NORFOLK TERMINAL OF THE SONOMA VALLEY PRISMOIDAL RY.
(As envisioned by the Stock Prospectus)

Coupled fore and aft of the locomotive were flat cars similarly contrived and on which Kohn had arranged benches for his guests. They, having come this far, felt they had to get aboard, but most of them did so with the secret belief that the whole affair would tumble over if the engine ever started.

But start it did, after a couple of very ordinary whistle blasts, echoed by somewhat tremulous cheers from the riders, and, surprisingly enough, it worked! As George Fogg, who had built the balancing behemoth at the Pacific Foundry, widened a bit on the throttle even the slight starting oscillation ironed out. A reporter from the

Alta noted that it rode quite as smoothly as the seven-foot gauge Great Western Railway in England, but possibly he exaggerated. Anyway, the trip was a huge success, and back aboard the *Sonoma,* en route home to their turkey dinners, the excursionists passed flowery resolutions of congratulations to Joe Kohn and his cohorts. The Sonoma Valley Prismoidal Railway, they opined, would go far.

It didn't. It never even reached Sonoma. It had one vital disadvantage not obvious during the three-mile jaunt through the tules. There was no practical solution for grade crossings. The little train operated for a few months while Kohn scratched his head at this dilemma. Then it folded up.

A new company, the Sonoma Valley Railroad, was formed by the directors in 1878 to replace it with a narrow gauge. Kohn converted himself from the prismoidal system simultaneously and as General Manager and Contractor remained. But when only a few miles of three-foot gauge track were laid, the contingency that Peter Donahue expected and was waiting for came to pass — funds ran out, and the Colonel took it over. When the "General Vallejo," flower bedecked by her namesake's family, hauled the first Sonoma train down Spain Street in front of the old Mission in December '79, the Sonoma Valley Railroad was another Donahue line — to be easily connected with his other properties.

In June, 1880, he gathered them all into one corporate entity. The San Francisco & North Pacific *Railway* Company was incorporated to absorb the *Railroad* Company plus the Sonoma & Marin Railway, the Fulton & Guerneville Railroad, and the Sonoma Valley Railroad. Almost immediately he was approached by an Eastern syndicate to sell out for three million dollars. They wanted to extend the system on up to Oregon. Peter Donahue was tempted to let them have it, but when he discovered that 90 per cent of the three millions would be in bonds, of which they planned to float five million with his property as security, he walked out in a hurry.

Reproduction of a portion of a North Pacific Coast advertising folder extolling the virtues of the land its trains traversed.

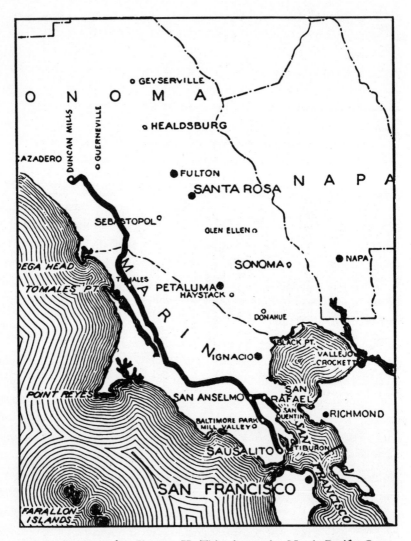

Orientation map for Chapter X. This shows the North Pacific Coast
almost at its zenith.

X

Luxury On A Slim Track

THE NORTH PACIFIC COAST, when it took over the San Rafael &
San Quentin Railroad in 1875, fulfilled the original subsidy require-
ment for a main line through the county seat of San Rafael. Its
release from this obligation by the supervisors two years before,
Coleman had maintained, was beyond their authority, and he had
brought a suit to hold up delivery of the bonds which was still pending. This issue removed, Milton Latham and his counsel had appeared before the board and again requested the railroad's $160,000.

But the county officials had found a new excuse. The 5 per cent
Act of 1870, under which the agreement had been made, had since
been repealed, so they claimed they had lost the power to issue the
bonds. In vain Latham stressed that repeal of a law had no effct on
contracts legally made under it while it was in force. The supervisors,
with the shadow of William Coleman's displeasure before them,
would not budge. The North Pacific Coast sued out a writ of man-
damus to compel the board to act. Just before Christmas of 1875
Judge Wallace upheld the writ on grounds of constitutional sanctity
of contracts. The supervisors appealed the decision to the Supreme
Court which sustained Judge Wallace the following April.

By that time, the quiet charm of Milton Latham had done much
to alter public feeling toward the narrow gauge. Many felt that had
he been president from the beginning there would have been no such

71

misunderstandings. The local press, which before had vigorously backed Coleman, agreed, and the *Herald* deplored the

> "subsidy farce . . . which through the smartness of some of our far-seeing (?) citizens, has so long been withheld [the bonds] . . . thereby crippling its business, retarding improvements, and putting back our town."

The bonds were issued with no further delay.

Latham was a perfectionist. A railroad should be an artistic triumph no less than the marbles and bronzes in his salon. He was determined that although the North Pacific Coast could not hope to develop into the railroad empire he had visualized for himself in his California Pacific days, yet it would lack for nothing in distinction. Peter Donahue had sent his palatial private car to edify the East at the Philadelphia Centennial Exposition. Latham had one delivered that outdid it in every department but gauge. To use it as a business car seemed on a par with standing the Venus de Milo in a drugstore window wearing a display of trusses. The parlor, flanked by a roomy observation platform, was paneled in rare inlaid woods, draped with heavy damask, and hung with a few of the sybaritic president's smaller canvasses. Relaxed on sofas and easy chairs, he and his guests watched countless redwoods broader than the car itself as the track picked its way through the groves, while steward Wan Sin padded back and forth from his culinary department forward with refreshing potables. Soon the China boy would spread a gourmet's banquet for them in the saloon. The rumbling wheels hushed by deep carpets, only the chandelier crystals tinkling around curves, and an occasional whistle from the locomotive, mingled with discourse on arts and letters as they savored Milton Latham's gracious living on the narrow gauge. Afterward, a "flick of the wrist" converted the saloon into four staterooms—as for the president, he had a master bedroom amidships, complete with four-poster and red marble commode.

To haul this noble vehicle the banker procured a special engine. Instead of common brass, her domes, bell and other trim were gleaming German silver, her cab solid burnished mahogany. Both car and locomotive were modestly named "Milton S. Latham." They bore his monogram in gold leaf filagree, but no other identification.

As to ferry service, he was determined that the North Pacific Coast should reign supreme. Stung by comments in the press which pictured weary passengers whiling away hours on the slow old *Petaluma of Saucelito* by singing "Do They Miss Me at Home, Do They Miss Me?" and "We are Coming, Blessed Savior!" or suggesting that she be fitted with staterooms and provisions for three days at sea, Latham journeyed East and contracted for two boats that would put the *James M. Donahue* and even the Oakland Ferries to shame. The N. P. C. had no funds for these so he paid for them himself. And he wanted them at once so had them shipped by rail!

The two great steamers, *Saucelito* and *San Rafael,* each 220 feet long and designed to carry 3,000 passengers, were built at Green Point, New York. Then they were carefully taken apart, each piece numbered, and packed in freight cars. One boat required 120 cars and the first, *San Rafael,* arrived over the Central Pacific in several special trains during March, 1877. She was rapidly reassembled at the Potrero and by July ready for her trial trip. With Latham and a few friends standing on her deck, no seats having been yet installed, she easily outran the *Donahue,* although, being unloaded, her buckets lacked four inches of normal dip.

Under command of Captain McKenzie who had opened the San Quentin run for Minturn with the old *Contra Costa,* the *San Rafael* went into service a month later. The Marin commuters almost purred in the soft cushioned seats of her "grand saloon" on the upper deck, while below, the "ladies' saloon" was a tired shopper's haven of easy chairs and soothing feminine luxury. All through the boat you could hear the ship's band, and not giving out with "We Are Coming, Blessed Savior," either. Outside, the paddle boxes sported more lace than the unmentionables blowing in the breeze on Barbary Coast clotheslines but, unlike them, were emblazoned with the Great Seal of California. Perched on the foremast a golden eagle spread his wings, exulting in speed that passed everything on the Bay. "The good people of San Rafael," warned the *Herald,* "will no longer submit to the supercilious airs of superiority of the conceited Oaklanders with meekness and humility." Running time across the bay was cut by fifteen minutes.

Two months later the *Saucelito* joined the N. P. C. fleet. Both fine steamers were to meet a tragic end.

During 1875 and '76, Latham had also extended his road from Tomales to the river which the Russians, for whom it was now called, had originally christened the Slavinka. Appropriately enough the terminal was Moscow. To a large extent he had financed the work himself and most of it was pretty heavy construction. Fifty-pound rail was laid instead of thirty-five-pound iron as on the older section. No expense was spared to make the North Pacific Coast the finest narrow gauge in California.

The new division maintained the road's allure for the tourist. On leaving Tomales, perhaps still speculating about the vacationing females who could be glimpsed briefly through the redwoods—some garbed as if for the Bella Union Stage — the conductor might show him Mt. St. Helena to the northeast and, if the day were exceptionally clear, the snow crested Sierras far beyond. Then the train climbed along a mountain side, thundered across a gulch called Estero Americano into Valley Ford; then paused at Freestone with its famous Julian's Hotel; shrieked around a giant horseshoes bend and out onto the dizzy double Howe truss which spanned Salmon Creek. Then through Summit tunnel into Howard's Station, which is now called Occidental, and downgrade into a redwood cathedral whose pillars dwarfed the cars. Along Dutch Bill Creek the train passed the Streeton and Tyrone Mills and followed the left bank of the Russian River three miles to the Moscow Mill. Both the Tyrone and the Moscow were properties of the Russian River Land and Lumber Company and, consequently, the prime reason for the railroad's being.

For years A. Duncan & Company had operated a huge mill at the river's mouth; this they moved to a new site near Moscow, and the railroad was extended across the river to serve it in May, 1877.

Here at the terminus in a lush meadow, encircled by a bend in the river and surrounded by forest covered mountains, an attractive village grew. Monsieur Julian moved his hotel from Freestone and between lumberjacks and city folks on holiday kept it full. Pietro's Restaurant and John Orr's saloon supplied vital facilities, while Duncan's Mill itself conducted a huge general store. Several hundred hunkies worked in the woods and mills, and often as many vacationists crowded the hotel and the tents around it.

Now, at last, the North Pacific Coast Railroad was ready to handle the lumber traffic for which it was projected, although it had taken an almighty round-about route to reach it, and a difficult, expensive one to work. The four big mills together could turn out 155,000 feet a day. Carried at $5.00 per thousand, that meant a tidy income for the narrow gauge — it would make the rest of its meager freight busines look like peanuts. However, the price of finished lumber in San Francisco chose this time to drop to a new low of $13.00 a thousand. To blame was the situation in the Northwest where gypo loggers were merrily denuding Government timber lands without a word to Uncle, and Puget Sound mill men with no sense of curiosity as to the source of the logs they bought, turned out unlimited lumber at little more cost than labor. The Russian River mills, priced out of the market, shut down. The traffic that remained for the N. P. C., remarked the Marin County *Tocsin,* could be handled by a two cat-power engine.

It was a body blow for the North Pacific Coast and proved a fatal one for Latham. By this time he had personally put up about half of the three and a quarter million spent on railroad, steamers and rolling stock. Rumors began to fly that the whole road north of San Rafael would be torn up and sold for junk. John Doherty, the superintendent, slashed service and raised fares with little result except oaths and maledictions from the commuters. The newest locomotive, the "Sonoma," was sold to the Nevada Central.

No interest had been paid on the bonds and the holders were about to sue. Latham tried to float a new, and much larger, issue but failed. He worked up a promising deal with an Eastern syndicate; they were going to form the San Francisco & Northern Railway to absorb the N. P. C., Latham's ferryboats, and the Russian River Land and Lumber Company, but their agent, Gibson Homan, died at the Palace Hotel just as the papers were ready to sign, and the bargain fell through.

Then Latham also passed away. The strain had been telling on him for years. He had resigned from the London & San Francisco Bank at the close of 1877 and gone to Europe for his health. Apparently restored, on his return, the same worries met him and now laid him low, his fortune vanished. During his absence, J. G. Eastland had been acting president — also a tragic, if short, administration, as his small daughter Ethel had lost her life when the fabulous private car jumped the track and rolled forty feet into Lagunitas Creek. Now John W. Doherty, Latham's general manager, succeeded to the office, while Warren Dutton, Moore, and the other principal stockholders, sought a way out from under the crushing debts.

The Northwest bootleg logging was eventually brought under control, and the Russian River mills began to turn again at near capacity. Things began to look a bit brighter for the narrow gauge. Lumber trains rolled and their revenue made nice black figures in the ledger that were good to look at.

A Central Pacific engineer, loaned to inspect the road for the San Francisco & Northern group, had reported that the N. P. C. was most informally operated. For example, a dairy up on White's Hill received feed in carload lots but there was no room on the slope for a siding. So when the afternoon passenger pulled into San Anselmo with a pair of boxcars coupled on behind, agent Albert Dutton (nephew of Warren) knew it was his cue to lock the depot and ride on up to the dairy. No. 13 would drop the feed cars on the main line and the cowboys would unload them. Then Albert would take his place at the leading brake wheel with a good stout club and ride the empties, screeching down the sinuous grade in darkness all the way to San Anselmo.

Firemen often had to perch out front on the pilot and lob chunks of coal, snitched from the ferryboat supply at Saucelito, at cows disputing the right of way. Mules seemed immune to both missiles and the curses that went with them in such disputes and were yanked off the track with chains hooked to the engine. Even when no pesty animals bothered, the tallowpot was busy jumping off to open gates at private sidings or racing up to the nearest ranch house for middlin's to grease his guides. On the Glorious Fourth, he helped his engineer slick up their old mill in an effort to outshine all the others: Chromos of Washington and Lincoln circled by redwood wreaths on the headlight, stack and boiler festooned with more evergreens, flowers and bunting, flags and rosettes on the cab and maybe a miniature cannon on the cowcatcher were considered a respectable showing.

Everyone had heard of White's Hill tunnel but few knew about the short bore that preceded it unless they had been over the line. Brakeman's delight was to yell "the train will be four minutes passing through the White's Hill tunnel!" just before the first one and then watch amatory couples and tilted flasks caught by the daylight a few seconds later.

Two kinds of passenger business were booming — the picnic and vacation trade, and the commuter haul to San Rafael and the new suburban hamlets springing up. But the narrow gauge was no longer to have a monopoly of the commuters. Peter Donahue incorporated the San Francisco & San Rafael Railroad in 1882 to extend his road to Point Tiburon, as close to the City by ferry as Saucelito and half the San Quentin run. The North Pacific Coast would have to further speed up its service or see Donahue get most of the commuters.

Doherty knew just what to do. Milton Latham had planned it all back in 1876. It was to reinstate Saucelito as the main ferry terminal but to cut out the long circuitous pull over Collins Summit by a tunnel at Corte Madera. The North Pacific Coast Railway Extension Company was formed to build it, but could not finance it. Finally Doherty found some English capital to build the tunnel, the railroad to pay toll on every passenger and ton of freight.

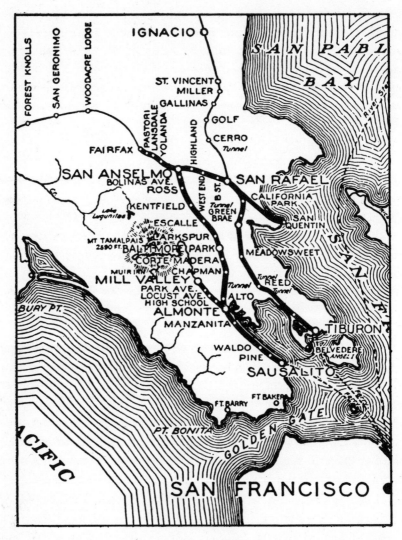

Orientation map for Chapter XI showing the commuter routes with
ferry connections.

The San Rafael "Union Depot" in the early '90s. S.F. & N.P. No. 8 SAN RAFAEL "pops off" as she waits a highball for the run to Tiburon.

A S.F. & N.P. train stops at the San Rafael Salt Water Baths in the '80s.

P. W. Tompkins

Ken Kidder

S.F. & N.P. No. 7 PETALUMA.

S.F. & N.P. train leaving Hopland, 1893

George Oliver

Roy D. Graves

S.F. & N.P. No. 5 SANTA ROSA. Built by San Francisco's Union Iron Works in 1873.

"Street Car Service" along the Russian River. Engine No. 99 "THE COFFEE GRINDER" and the coach MONSANO.

Point Tiburon, the terminus of the San Francisco and North Pacific Railway, showing the steamers *Ukiah, James M. Donahue* and *Tiburon,* (plying between Tiburon and San Francisco, 6.50 miles), and part of yard.

The ill-fated North Pacific Coast ferry *San Rafael*.

Pride of the San Francisco & North Pacific, the ferry *Tiburon*.

The North Pacific Coast trains were dwarfed by the trees they invaded.

S.F. & N.P. No. 10 HEALDSBURG and train leaving Tiburon in the '90s.

XI

Commuter Handicap

NOW THAT the chips were down, the two roads raced to be first in offering expedited commuter service. Peter Donahue had the larger task, but he had greater resources and a more efficient staff. There were three tunnels to dig on his Tiburon line and a bad stretch of marsh where trainload after trainload of rock ballast sank without a trace. At Point Tiburon itself the hills slanted steep into the Bay, and acres of shelf for shops, round-house, yards and the like, had to be chiseled out. For this the old Colonel procured a brand new invention — a steam shovel just patented at Bucyrus, Ohio. The new-fangled machine loaded a whole car in three minutes and folks flocked to watch — many muttering that the foul contraption took bread out of honest workingmen's mouths.

The rival roads came down the finish stretch cowcatcher and cowcatcher. Both were ready, except for their tunnels, by February, 1884. Donahue, with three steam drills working around the clock in the last of his smokeholes, saw daylight glimmer through on March 10th; the North Pacific Coast only six days later.

The narrow gauge caught up during the finishing touches and managed to route trains over its new line two days before the S. F. & N. P. started to use the Tiburon line on April 28th. The N. P. C. opened its new service with little showmanship, but Peter Donahue liked to throw a party, complete with champagne and reporters whenever there was any excuse. On May Day he rode several hundred guests over from the City on the *James M. Donahue.* (His new double-ended *Tiburon,* powered with an engine he'd built in 1860, was about to be launched at the Fulton Iron Works.)

At Tiburon, previously known as Lyford's Hygeia, because one Dr. Benjamin Lyford went there after the Civil War to die but found himself restored to health, the new terminal was impressive. "Everything suggests the ferry of a continental route, rather than the mere outlet of a new county's commerce" wrote a modest Rafaelite. The slip into which they coasted was a marvel of 1,280 piles modeled on the latest New York ferry practice, and the buildings were trim and substantial. In the train shed stood six yellow coaches, glistening in their virgin varnish, and all brand new. To haul them steamed the "Ukiah," also just delivered, from the Union Iron Works, and shined to dazzling brightness.

At San Rafael most of the local denizens, plus a large group that had come down on the morning train from all along the line, jammed into the unfinished depot at Fourth and Tamalpais Avenue as the festive train puffed in. After some brassy music, Mayor Saunders welcomed the party and eulogized the brilliant career of Peter Donahue from his founding of the Union Iron Works in 1849 onward. The Colonel's response might be taken as a good model for such occasions:

> "I feel deeply the complimentary things you have said in reference to myself and the enterprise we are now inaugurating, and I scarcely know how to thank you and the people of your town and county who are now present. But I desire to say that I entered upon this enterprise in a business point of view. I thought, and I think now, that there is something in it for me, and I am fully convinced that the best way to make it remunerative to me is to do that which will be pleasing and satisfactory to you. And so I propose to carry you safely, speedily and pleasantly to and from your handsome little town, and I propose to do it cheaply. I want you all to ride with me, but I want you to pay your fare. As business increases, as I think it will, I will reduce rates, because while I wish to live myself, I am willing that you shall live also. We had intended to have a little

collation here today, but our depot is not completed, and in this we are disappointed, but if you will all get aboard of the cars we will take you to Petaluma and bring you back. We have sandwiches and wine enough for the ladies and whiskey enough for the men. Get aboard—quick!"

On the train, J. Mervyn Donahue, twenty-five year old newlywed son of the president, functioned as master of ceremonies. He kept the champagne and whiskey flowing and saw that no one's throat was dry, including his own. Folks liked his democratic friendliness — they were glad he and his bride had chosen to live among them in San Rafael.

Colonel Donahue established low-cost commutes — $5.00 monthly for a man; $8.00 if he wanted his wife included. The North Pacific Coast, perforce, announced the same rates. The S. F. & N. P. ran five trips daily, the narrow gauge six. Doherty abandoned the San Quentin ferry, but ran a train or two to the Point to serve the prison. Both lines were on their mettle and the intense rivalry that started lasted into the next century. The Rafaelites were a little dazed at first. "We have been a sleepy people so long that many are nervous at the rate of speed" explained a *Journal* man after riding the cars at twenty-five miles an hour. But soon jitters were forgotten and the commuters themselves grew fiercely partisan.

If hubby, who patronized Donahue's "Irishman's Railroad," couldn't eat his dinner, the wife knew without dangerous questions that the *San Rafael* and connecting narrow gauge "Flyer" had outstripped the *Tiburon* and her train that evening. Broad gauge riders liked to mention the Hobbs automatic couplers with which Donahue had just equipped his cars. Their trains were made up without toll in brakemen's fingers, they bragged. Narrow gauge men retorted with the merits of N. P. C. Miller platform-buffers and air brakes. Or perhaps didn't speak to the enemy at all. Racing was, of course, strictly banned by the rules of both railroads. Doherty hung five demerits on a ferry captain caught in the act — ten if he lost to the broad gauge boat.

The Tiburon line was such a success that the San Francisco & North Pacific decided to abandon its terminal at Donahue. The buildings were all loaded on barges and floated to Tiburon where the giant steam shovel had scooped out a few more acres for them.

As for the North Pacific Coast, despite its new speedy route and growing business, it was still having its troubles. The loss of Latham's fine new *Saucelito* was a bitter blow. Tied up at San Quentin one Sunday night, just before the switch in service, and renovated and overhauled in preparation, the ship's bootblack who lived aboard upset his oil lamp in a drunken stupor. Flames spread quickly and licked at the graceful white superstructure. A wire to Superintendent Shoemaker brought the San Rafael Volunteer Fire Department on a special train, but it was too late. Firemen and railroaders tried to scuttle her to save the engines, then to get her away and save the wharf. At risk of life they cut her loose and shoved her off; a cynical tide swung her back just long enough to doom the pier and then an offshore breeze came up and swept her in her shroud of flame to sea, a total loss. The bootblack was a total loss also.

More basic were the financial and management problems. Ever since Latham's death, the major stockholders had been anxious to get out from under the crushing debts its carried. Contemporary corporation law held them individually liable for their proportion and faced them with ruin in the event of a foreclosure. By 1881 these debts totaled $2,400,000 as follows:

London and San Francisco Bank	$400,000
Bank of British Columbia	160,000
Société Mutuelle des Epargnes (French Bank)	940,000
Clay Street Bank	300,000
Latham estate	600,000

They had made continual efforts to find someone who would accept their stock as a gift, with the further inducement that the debtors would take 50¢ on the dollar. Some of them had actually retained the well-known corporation lawyer, A. A. Cohen, and sent him East in the search, but he hadn't turned up anyone that anxious to own a railroad. Finally Warren Dutton took over for the mobilized share-holders and, early in 1884, made a deal with James D. Walker, one of the original promoters of the San Rafael and San Quentin. Walker, who had replaced Latham as head of the London and San Francisco Bank, agreed in the bank's name to accept the stock, gladly turned over gratis, and to assume responsibility for the scaled-down indebtedness. The transaction made no hit with the British owners of the bank, and they gave Walker the sack but made him president of the North Pacific Coast. He had saddled them with a white elephant — now let him run it!

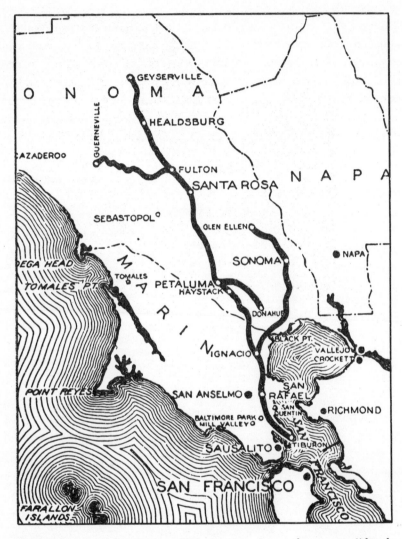

Orientation map for Chapter XII showing the roads as consolidated by Mervyn Donahue.

XII

The King is Dead!

IN NOVEMBER OF '85, aging Peter Donahue spent a blustery day inspecting his Tiburon terminal. The wind howled through the Gate, cold and raw, and he was snuffling heavily when he came home to the old Rincon Hill mansion at Second and Bryant where he'd lived a quarter century. Annie, his wife, hustled him into bed with a mustard plaster, but nine days later he reached the end of his track. Fate of the S. F. & N. P. among the three heirs — widow, son, and his "little girl," who had already fulfilled the American millionaire's daughter's destiny by becoming Baroness von Schroeder — seemed headed for litigation, but an amicable settlement was finally reached in which Mervyn took the railroad.

J. Mervyn Donahue, like his father a colonel in the California National Guard, was a very amiable young man, as he had shown on the Tiburon excursion, but he lacked the background of elemental struggle that breeds strength of character. The spring years that Peter spent pounding out the beginnings of a fortune with sledge and bellows in a tent, his son enjoyed on the campuses of St. Ignatius, Santa Clara and England's Stonehurst. He was, in the day's phrase, "a jolly good fellow" — a commuter on the cocktail route and an enthusiastic fan of the gas-lit decadence that was San Francisco's night life. Nevertheless, he had immense pride in the San Francisco & North Pacific Railway and was firmly determined to carry out his father's plans for its destiny.

85

The first dilemma that faced him was a minor revolt by the Santa Rosans. They were tired of being without through train connections with the rest of the United States. It all came to a head in a Court House mass meeting in the summer of 1886. One faction wanted to proposition the Central Pacific; another felt Donahue should be consulted first. The upshot was they decided to build their own railroad and organized the Santa Rosa & Benicia Central Railroad Company to connect with the C. P., or Southern Pacific as the whole Big Four system was now called.

A third of the million dollar capital was soon subscribed, though rumor had Mervyn Donahue requesting his friends to stay out. The S. R. & B. C. hired the well known railroad engineer Colonel Lyman Bridges, but before he could set up a transit, the trio still left of the Big Four pushed into the scene with a proposition. For a measly $40,000 subsidy they would build the road. The Santa Rosans joyfully turned over their enterprise and the cash subscribed to date. Stanford and Crocker incorporated the Santa Rosa & Carquinez Railroad Company and sent their chief engineer William Hood, but characteristically didn't let him start until the entire subsidy was in their pockets.

Young Colonel Donahue was not pleased at this activity in what he fondly thought of as his own backyard. He filed papers for a Sonoma Valley Extension Railroad to link Santa Rosa with Glen Ellen, terminal of his S. V., but it was generally dismissed as a bluff. There were many who did not expect the gay, youthful socialite would hang on to his own railroad very long.

The playboy, however, was not tickling his toes with grass growing under his feet. He had made connections with the Seligmans — big New York bankers — which assured adequate capital for expansion. He formed the Marin & Napa Railroad to link the Sonoma Valley line with the S. F. & N. P. at Ignacio — a costly seven miles on piles and fill through the tules — and the Cloverdale & Ukiah Railroad to build thirty miles north from his father's terminal. The people of the Mendocino County Seat had agreed to furnish free right-of-way and ground for a depot and Donahue signed a formal agreement to have the road running in eighteen months for this consideration. It would be the heaviest construction yet on the San Francisco & North Pacific line — most of it through the rugged canyon of the upper Russian River.

The S. P. started running trains over their new line from Napa Junction in May, but not until a month later was the official opening staged. That day saw huge crowds jamming the Santa Rosa horsecars, walking, driving toward the new depot. There was a grand procession with bands, artillery, floats, and bigwigs in decorated buggies — a far cry from the chilly greeting accorded the first S. F. & N. P. train eighteen years before.

An hour behind schedule the "first" Southern Pacific trains pulled in. Mark McDonald of Sonoma brandished a silver hammer three times around his head to cheers and then drove the gold spike on which Shreve's had carved "Santa Rosa and Carquinez Railroad— June 20, 1888." Locomotives screamed, and the ubiquitous bands obliged some more. An unsung genius has committed the occasion to undying verse:

> See! the clogging wheels grind sullenly beneath the brakes—
>   they slow!
> Stop! the dying engine's polished bands throw back the sunset's
>   glow!
> The valves are wide—the halted train is wrapped in steamy veil,
> And the ponderous mass of iron stands upon the final rail.
>
>   *   *   *   *   *
>
> Oh, Sonoma! Land of Luna! let me lengthen my refrain!
> Let me weave thy bloom and beauty in the texture of my strain.

No encouragement being evident for the offer to "lengthen my refrain," the crowd dispersed toward the barbecue at Kroncke's Park.

Three weeks before, young Donahue had opened his Marin & Napa Railroad. He closed down the ferry to Sonoma Landing, all passengers going via Tiburon. The M. & N. was standard gauge, but soon a third rail carried the narrow gauge Sonoma Valley trains to the junction at Ignacio.

With work progressing nicely on his Ukiah extension, the young Colonel, still smarting under the Southern Pacific's triumphal entry into Santa Rosa, journeyed to Humboldt Bay. Here the thirty-mile Eel River & Eureka Railroad ran southward, a natural link in a through San Francisco & North Pacific line, but when he broached the matter of purchase he was shocked to find the S. P. already had it under option. Was the Santa Rosa & Carquinez but a step in a Southern Pacific branch to Humboldt Bay? S. P. surveyors, too, were running lines from Winters via Clear Lake to Ukiah, from Willows to Eel River, and only God and the deer in the hills knew where else. The empire that Peter Donahue had built was under siege from the same Central Pacific crowd who had sluffed it off as worthless fifteen years before.

Mervyn Donahue had listened to the tale of Asbury Harpending. He was familiar with the story of Milton Latham and his ambitions for the California Pacific. Both had stirred the Big Four to alarmed buzzing like bees in an upset hive with their plans to cross the Sierras. The young Colonel proceeded to wangle a franchise, Oroville through Beckwourth Pass, and let it "leak out" that he planned to extend his Marin & Napa northeastward through the Sacramento Valley and the mountains. With the Seligmans behind him, this could not safely be laughed off as a playboy's pipe dream. The Santa Rosa & Carquinez went no further, and the Eel River & Eureka option was allowed to die. The playboy had outfoxed the old masters at their own game.

STEAMER "City of Lakeport"

Running in Con-
nection with the
SAN FRANCISCO & NORTH PACIFIC RY.
For the following
points on
CLEAR LAKE

Bartlett Landing, Soda Bay, Cape Floyd, Paradise Valley, Sulphur

Banks, Buckinghams, Kanocti, and Lower Lake

On and After Monday, May 15, 1890, the above steamer will run as follows:

Leave Lower Lake (Gruell's Stage Line)..............at 6.00 A. M.
" Lower Lake Landing....................................at 6.30 A. M.

Stopping (when signaled or to leave passengers) at Kanocti, Buckinghams, Sulphur Banks, Paradise Valley, Cape Floyd, Soda Bay, and arriving at Bartlett Landing at 9.45 A. M. to take Bartlett Springs passengers.

Leave Bartlett Landing..at 10.00 A. M.
Arrive at Lakeport...at 10.45 A. M

making close connection with C., O. and I. Co's stages for Hopland; arriving in San Francisco at 7 20 P. M.

Leave Lakeport (on arrival of C., O. and I Co's Stages) 4.10 P. M., stopping at Bartlett Landing to leave Bartlett Springs passengers, and at Soda Bay, Cape Floyd, Paradise Valley, Sulphur Banks, Buckinghams and Kanocti (when signaled or to leave passengers), arriving at Lower Lake at 7.30 P. M.

Fare between San Francisco and any of the above-named points, **$6.00.**

☞ Until May 15, 1890, the steamer "City of Lakeport" will leave Lakeport for the above landings every Tuesday, Thursday and Saturday at 9.30 A. M.

This is by far the pleasantest route to Seigler and Adam Springs. By this route passengers go by water almost the entire length of Clear Lake, and stop at all points of interest. Tickets can be had at

Tiburon Ferry, Foot of Clay St.
(Next to Oakland Ferry

No. 222 Montgomery St. (California Transfer Co's Office)

SPECIAL NOTICE—Until May 15, 1890, Passengers for **Lower Lake** and way land-ings will leave San Francisco, via Tiburon Ferry, foot of Clay St., at **7.40 A. M.** on Mondays, Wednesdays and Fridays, and lay over night at Lakeport, taking steamer the following morning at **9.00 A. M.** for Lower Lake and way landings.

S.F.& N.P.

Advertisement from Bancroft's Railway Guide of May, 1890. The "connection" with the S. F. & N. P. was via a rather lengthy stage coach ride.

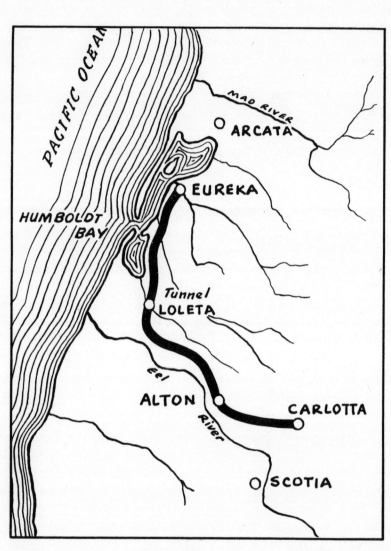

Orientation map for Chapter XIII showing the Humboldt County
operations.

XIII

Iron Horses at Humboldt Bay

THE EEL RIVER & EUREKA RAILROAD, however, is still to play an important role in this chronicle, so let's get better acquainted with it.

Long before General Pat Connor had promoted the San Francisco & Humboldt Bay Railroad in 1868, the people of Humboldt County had been railroad conscious. In fact, they claimed the State's first railway, for back in 1854, when Captain Ulysses S. Grant of Fort Humboldt was trying to forget his loneliness and the wretched climate in Eureka's numerous bars, twenty miles of primitive but substantial logging railroad was in use. The Union Wharf and Plank Walk Company also had a line to Arcata — motive power, an aged white horse named "Spanking Fury."

Not many years later, John Vance, a hulking, blunt Nova Scotian ship's carpenter, who had come soon after Connor but had stayed and become a big redwood operator, proposed to link Eureka with Eel River Valley, if he could have a subsidy and a free right-of-way, but the former was voted down. Then, during the last year of the Civil War, an oil boom brought derricks springing up like mushrooms fifty miles south, and the idea came up again. This time stock came from the engravers and engineers were hired, but before they could even establish a bench mark the boom collapsed leaving no trace but a village named Petrolia.

Vance placed his proposition on the ballot again in 1871; this time frankly as a link in the eventual main line to San Francisco, but again the Eurekans said "no subsidy!" with a whopping vote. Six years later there was another flurry. Some of the merchants had begun to wonder if Vance, William Carson, and the other lumber magnates, were not actually working against a railroad southward in order to prevent the more distant redwood groves coming into competition with their properties. Some hot meetings were held at Eureka's Centennial Hall, and there was much palaver about subsidies, lumber barons, prismoidal railways and the like, but nothing happened.

More than likely the merchants had grounds for their suspicions, for when action finally came it was forced by alien invaders of the redwood realm. Paxton and Curtis with their Austin, Nevada silver, and the further support of the Anglo-California Bank, had formed The Pacific Lumber Company and secured an extensive virgin grove on the Eel River at what is now Scotia. For quite a while they remained undecided on how to get their lumber to market. They purchased Henye's Landing and then seemed to vacillate between building a railroad to it or to the south peninsula of Humboldt Bay.

Either would have been painful to Eureka, so the pioneer lumber tycoons forgot their stalling about subsidies and organized the Eel River & Eureka Railroad to protect their city's status and to insure their own control of any road which could be incorporated into a through line. John Vance would be vice-president and general manager; William Carson, president. A preliminary survey was made during the summer of '82, followed by incorporation in November. For a while it looked as though Paxton and the Anglo-California Bank people would not come to terms with the locals — they still talked of constructing their own railroad to Humboldt Bay and even tried to buy out the Eel River & Eureka. Finally they accepted the situation and agreed to build only to a junction with the latter, although they christened their road the Humboldt Bay & Eureka.

Construction of the E. R. & E. commenced at Field's Landing, a small port on the south arm of Humboldt Bay, fifty minutes from Eureka via the stern-wheeler *Oneatta.* Between the Bay and Eel River Valley, Table Bluff ridge called for a 2,000-foot tunnel under a cemetery, thence the line wound up the Eel River to its junction with the Van Duzen and along that stream to Hydesville. Vance started gangs on both sides of Table Bluff and ordered day and night shifts in the tunnel. The first of the pair of locomotives he had ordered from Baldwin arrived in May, 1884. Down at Newark, Carter Brothers' new factory was turning out two coaches and a combine, both with reversible perforated wooden seats, ten box cars, and thirty flats.

The Eel River & Eureka Railroad was opened for business between Field's Landing and Hydesville on November 24, 1884. There was no celebration—Eureka had celebrated itself out at Grover Cleveland's election two nights before. But a large crowd boarded the *Oneatta* from the old City Wharf at the foot of F Street and transferred to the shiny new cars at Field's. A huge stack of rails was evidence there would soon be track to Eureka. The train stopped briefly at Salmon Creek, reached the Table Bluff tunnel where the engineer Jim Townsend pushed in the throttle and crawled slowly through the smoke hole, plunged out into the sunshine again and past Singley's Ferry across the Eel, Springville, Rohnerville, and Drakes. The track stopped at Burnell's, a mile short of Hydesville, but a stage was ready to close this gap. From Eureka, the twenty-five-mile jaunt had consumed two hours and fifty minutes.

By the following July, the track was finished into Eureka, and the city fathers laid a plank down Second Street to reach the new depot. No swinking Chinamen were seen on this railroad job. E and F Streets had long been Chinatown—a cluttered region of laundries and joss houses rocked by endless tong wars. The Eurekans, like other Californians, had no interest or objection when the Celestials chose to bump each other off. But in February, an American had been killed by a "hatchet man's" wild bullet. Thereupon all the Chinese in town were given forty-eight hours to leave for good. Two ships happened to be in the Bay, both were commandeered by vigilantes, and one assigned to each of the rival tongs. Many a Eurekan had argued himself hoarse to keep a well trained houseboy or cook, but a posse went from door to door, and none were spared. The two vessels sailed for San Francisco, and for years Humboldt advertised itself as the County with no Chinese.

The omission of an opening celebration in November was to be rectified by two excursions in July. The first, under the sedate auspices of the Excelsior Lyceum, left the dripping fog of Eureka early on the morning of the 24th with 850 sunshine-seeking picnickers crowded on fourteen flats. John Vance, William Carson, and other brass hats followed in the passenger equipment a little later, prepared to hear praise for the railroad but heard more about the naked boys caught bathing in the slough by the unexpected train and the shocked "we-mustn't-let-it-happen-agains" of the serious-minded Lyceumites.

The second excursion, a few days later, turned out an even larger crowd. A few demijohns were sneaked aboard, but no feminine headgear seemed disarranged at the other end of the tunnel, nor after luncheon in the pepperwood grove did any one, apparently, find more spicy diversion than the sonorous "inspirational" declaimed by Reverend Bowman. Picnic trains in Humboldt, it appeared, differed greatly from those nearer San Francisco. Perhaps folks there absorbed the somber shadings of their climate.

Meanwhile The Pacific Lumber Company had completed its seven-mile line from Scotia mill to the E. R. & E. junction, soon christened Alton in honor of the nearest farmer's daughter. Two train crews handled all the service on the Eel River & Eureka. One, based at Hydesville, made a morning passenger run to Eureka, then a round trip mixed, and finally, passenger home in the evening. The other crew tied up at South Bay and handled freight, principally lumber trains whose cars strained under a single log from Alton. The mixed train, with its interminable station stops, bred passenger frustration. It soon ceased to be funny when itchy riders asked conductor John McCann if the train was waiting for a farmer to finish milking. But it was a good little road — well built, well equipped, and well run, if a bit informally. The men of Southern Pacific, no doubt, hated to let their option die.

L. Stine

Eel River & Eureka No. 1 at Eureka.

Eel River & Eureka ferry *Oneatta*. Used to carry passengers from its terminal at Field's Landing before the road was extended to Eureka.

L. Stine

E.R. & E. No. 1 **EEL RIVER** with a train load of logs at Eureka.

Depot of the Eel River & Eureka Railroad at Fortuna.

E.R. & E. train crossing the Van Duzan River trestle.

Fourth of July, 1884, on the Humboldt & Mad River Railroad.

The Humboldt Logging Railway at Freshwater, just east of Eureka. The 24 redwood log sections with which the two trains on the left are loaded total 137,000 board feet.

Advertisement from the Ukiah *Dispatch and Democrat*, April 6, 1888.
This house was to be raffled to raise money for the right-of-way fund.

95

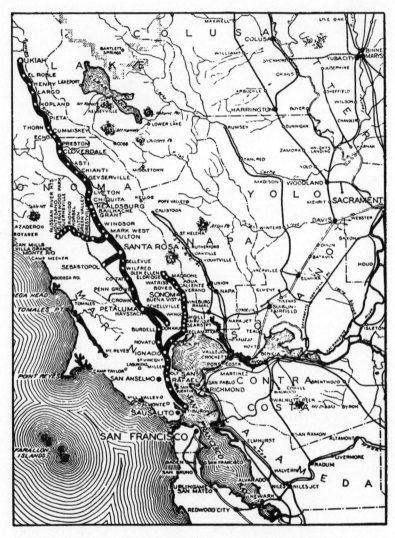

Orientation map for Chapter XIV showing the S. F. & N. P. completed
to Ukiah.

XIV

The Rails Reach Ukiah

RELYING ON the promise of Ukiah to finance the right-of-way, Mervyn Donahue filled the Russian River canyon with echoes of construction. But the Ukians were having troubles. At first, popular subscriptions had come in well; then the '87 hop and wool crops failed and with their two chief industries on the rocks, bankruptcy stalked farmer and merchant. To forestall the added disaster of seeing their railroad hopes go a-glimmering, local leaders formed the Ukiah Improvement Association to make up the arrears.

They chose a novel method — raffle of a house and lot. A two-story home — eleven rooms and bath — on a large corner lot at Hortense and Smith Streets was the prize. Five thousand tickets, to sell for $2.00 apiece, were printed, and each bore twenty numbers corresponding to those of the Louisiana State Lottery; the drawing at New Orleans, April 10th, would also decide the lucky Ukian. All proceeds to go to the right-of-way fund.

A lawyer named Hamilton had been a most faithful plugger throughout the whole right-of-way drive, and the Improvement Association put him in charge of its sweepstakes. Chances sold well, but the population was a bit sparse to absorb 5,000, and Hamilton put a large block in his grip and went down to the City to peddle them. He did not return. Last reports reaching the outraged committee and his deserted family placed him on a ship bound for Australia, money-belted with the lottery "take" in cozy double eagles.

97

A light winter carried the new track rapidly north through Hopland and toward Ukiah. As the short days of January faded, the townspeople drove out to see the gap steadily shorten. Then on the 9th of February, 1889, the rails were all laid, and Mervyn Donahue, Henry Whiting, his general manager, Frank Zook, chief engineer, and the rest of his official family, came up in his father's flamboyant old private car to drive the last spike. The young Colonel was drinking no less as the years and miles rolled by, an amazing quantity of Simmon's Nabob Bourbon had disappeared during the trip north. He felt it, just a little, as he stood poised with a spike maul — or maybe it was only dizziness from all the curves. He glanced down at the rail. Wasn't it slightly irregular to have two gold spikes? Anyhow, he'd better hit them both. The maul descended. So did young Colonel Donahue. Peacefully, he passed out on the track.

Hours later, he was able to respond graciously from a balcony at the Grand Hotel to the Ukiah Silver Band's serenade.

After a few days, a more extensive and slightly less alcoholic celebration was staged by the Ukiah Right-of-Way Committee in honor of its two-year successful effort. The Committee and the Silver Band met the special train at Cloverdale. No. 12, the "Peter Donahue," was at the smoky end and the five coaches and private car behind carried most of the wealth and much of the glamor of San Francisco.

The young Colonel was in much better shape. The "Peter Donahue" chuffed merrily around the curves beside the twisting, churning Russian River; the sun put on its best summer-in-February act; the Silver Band gave out with sterling music, and all was jovial aboard. Artillery boomed as they pulled into the packed Ukiah station grounds and carriages were ready to take visitors and hosts to Reed's Hall where over two hundred covers were laid for the grand banquet.

There were the usual champagne toasts and the usual speeches. Father Waugh of Petaluma displayed the invitation sent him by Peter Donahue to the first San Francisco & San Jose train back in '64. Now he had ridden the first train to Ukiah where he used to hunt bears. W. D. Sink boasted that he had also been on the first stage-coach up the valley. Progress had come with open throttle.

But late rains put the new line out of commission almost at once, and regular service to Ukiah did not start until April 15th. The mails, however, were carried through on a handcar.

The S. F. & N. P. undertook to make its new terminal the wool center of northwestern California. If sheep men would furnish esti-mates of their expected clips and delivery date in Ukiah, the railroad would notify buyers and arrange sales. It was a good idea, but wool was passing as the primary local crop. During the next year it ac-counted for only two per cent of the freight and less thereafter.

The San Francisco & North Pacific Railroad was now clearing about a quarter million dollars a year. Its freight business accounted for a little less than half its gross receipts and was extremely well diversified. Of twenty-three classifications, wine, the largest, brought in only 8½ per cent of freight revenue, although nine forest products items together totalled 17 per cent. Passenger business grossed around $400,000 and was well spread over the road. Picnic trains and excursions accounted for less than 5 per cent of this, but originated 95 per cent of the headaches.

Orientation map for Chapter XV showing the picnic routes that became the "Triangle Trip."

XV

Picnics Were No Picnic!

PICNICS AND EXCURSIONS of City characters had been a headache to Marin and Sonoma since the early '60s when San Rafael Day was in its doubtful glory. The railroads had spread the nuisance over the calendar and the countryside. Only a few days after the North Pacific Coast had opened in 1875, the first Sunday excursion train was run. The Union Guard, a San Francisco military outfit, hired it and the new picnic grounds at Fairfax. Innocent locals with an eye to a little spare change prepared to vend home-grown goodies to the visitors.

There were about 3,000 picnickers on that first excursion, of all shades and descriptions. How many were actually Guards is not recorded, but that they were almost all, male and female, thugs and savages, the Marin folk were convinced. The "picnic" was one grand drunken shindy with wenching and assorted larceny unfettered as the birds, who promptly left. The merrymakers overwhelmed the neat little refreshment stands provided by the Railroad, devoured all their edibles, and then kicked them into kindling wood in front of the trembling hucksters. A Portugese brought buttermilk from his nearby dairy — it was at once appropriated and the owner beaten up by those who didn't get any. An old codger with a basket of oranges suffered a like fate. The gay merrymakers didn't beat him much, in deference to his age, but took clubs to a stray Samaritan who tried to reimburse the old fellow for his stolen fruit and left *him* almost dead. It was a very full rural Sabbath.

This first Sunday excursion set the pitch for hundreds that were to follow and to plague the North Pacific Coast and the San Francisco & North Pacific for many years. San Francisco was not a sissy town, and its toughest characters enjoyed nothing more than a day of innocent mayhem and carnality in the country air. The roads soon fixed up flat cars for the picnic trains. They had too few coaches to haul these hordes and had learned through sad experience that even head-on collisions were apt to leave the rolling stock in better shape.

The brawls were not confined to excursion trains and picnic grounds. The tranquil towns along the railroads often suffered too. Santa Rosa was invaded one Sunday in '88 by a train load of Barbary Coasters and their lay brothers and sisters, who prowled the streets, spat in people's faces, insulted the local womenfolk, and knocked senseless anyone whose looks they didn't like. Shills staged sham fights for pickpockets who frisked the crowds that gathered, while Santa Rosa urchins hanging around the picnic grounds had no trouble learning what came after the birds and bees. The town marshal was helpless in the face of such odds, and to avoid another such onslaught, Mayor Byington appointed most of the men in town reserve cops, widely proclaimed that next time such goings on meant hard labor on the rock pile.

Superintendent Whiting of the S. F. & N. P. decided to see for himself what the holiday trains were like. He swung aboard a howling picnic special at San Rafael one Sunday morning just in time to see two decent youths who had made the mistake of coming have their arms broken for appearing to high-hat the general ribaldry. The trip back was worse. In one car a coterie of hooligans tossed their scintillating witticisms across the aisle toward a foursome of dubious maidens. One of the damsels sassed them back. Whereupon two of the toughs pinned her to the seat while the rest removed her drawers, the whole gang serpentining through the train waving the panties and asking every woman if they were hers. But let the conductor tell it:

> "Interfere! Well, I'm only one man and there were fully 600 toughs on board; but I would have taken the chances of a beating

and interfered when I saw the way they handled the girl, only the language she used convinced me that her modesty was not particularly outraged, and I did not see the use of killing a hoodlum or being killed myself to spare the blushes of a girl whose language made *me* blush.

There is nothing in this hoodlum picnic business anyway. The company has to keep a man all the time to arrange with the societies. The society appoints a committee, generally about a dozen members. Our man has to take this committee over the road to the picnic grounds, feed them and wine them, and make as much fuss over them as a candidate does over a bunch of delegates. Then we have to haul the crowd about 100 miles at a dollar a head and give the Society 25% rebate. People who would pay full fare anyhow go on the cheap trips and besides that it hurts the regular business of the road. And after a picnic our cars have to go to the shops to be repaired."

With this off his chest, the conductor made for home and an alcohol rub. But the picnic specials continued.

Of course, by no means all those who rode the N. P. C. and S. F. & N. P. on pleasure bent were of this ilk. The narrow gauge served many exclusive resorts and camps near the old paper mill at Lagunitas and in the Russian River country, while the Donahue line carried untold thousands of gaping tourists and the City's more conventional folk vacation-bound to the redwoods, or by connecting six-horse canopy-top thoroughbrace stages to The Geysers, Skagg's Springs, and Clear Lake across whose smooth waters the steamers *City of Lakeport* and *Bay City* bore them to even more remote retreats.

Most elite of all, perhaps, were the Bohemian Club members who rode up to their new Russian River redwood grove and added spice to their vocabularies by eavesdropping on the drivers of 12-ox lumber teams as they leapt, like Eliza crossing the ice, from ox to ox to goad delinquent bovines.

Orientation map for Chapter XVI showing the S. F. & N. P. with proposed extension as taken over by A. W. Foster.

104

XVI

The Prince Dies Too

MERVYN DONAHUE, like his father, died in the service of the road. A personal reconnaissance on foot, camping in the damp December woods with his engineers, planning the route north of Ukiah, left him with a cold — past indulgence, probably, allowed it to develop into complications of the lungs and stomach. For two months he lay ill at the Palace Hotel where marital difficulties had caused him to make his abode. Then, on the evening of March 3, 1890, he passed away. He was still only thirty.

The storm-drenched crowds outside Old St. Mary's blocked California Street completely as the great bell tolled his funeral. His National Guard regiment paraded, with arms reversed, to the Dead March from Saul. A huge flag kept his casket dry; his sheathed sword rested on it, and a seven-block long procession of somber carriages followed him to interment beside his father. Both had been greatly beloved by San Francisco.

Mervyn Donahue's will took the railroad out of the family. His first two children had died; a third was but a year old. He had already given his wife a large settlement, and she received no bequest. His entire estate, except for some minor cash legacies, was left to the Archbishop of San Francisco for an old people's home. It meant the sale at auction of the San Francisco & North Pacific. One of the cash bequests was for a suitable monument to Peter Donahue. It stands today in the gore at Market, Bush and Battery.

The directors selected Donahue's confidential secretary, John Burgin, to act as president pending action of the probate court. It was decided, as a matter of course, to proceed with all the young Colonel's unfinished projects—the $200,000 ferry *Ukiah* almost ready for launching, the purchase of three more locomotives and other needed rolling stock, standard gauging of the Sonoma Valley, only a month from completion, and the construction of the Ukiah-Calpella extension for which he had given his life. His six-mile branch to Sebastopol had just been opened.

For three years Burgin ran the S. F. & N. P. for the executors of the estate, with the help of the old Donahue staff — Whiting, Zook, Peter McGlynn, and the others — while the court deliberated, and he did it well. The old high standards were maintained. The Guerne-Murphy lumber railroad was bought to extend the Russian River branch. Local industry was encouraged with generous sidetracks — particularly the many new canneries. Iron rails were replaced with steel. Most important of all, perhaps, was the establishment of a Southern Pacific interchange at Schellville. Strangely enough, the tracks of the two railroads had never been connected at Santa Rosa. Reconnaissance was proceeding toward Booneville, Lakeport, and Eureka.

In February, 1893, the Superior Court of Marin County ordered the 42,000 Donahue shares sold at auction in the administration of the estate. In San Rafael lived one A. W. Foster, who had been watching carefully for this announcement. Another Irishman, he had worked for a New York broker house and first saw California when he was sent after an absconding fellow employee. Returning the offender to judgement, he had come back to stay. Now, in addition to his San Francisco brokerage house, he owned three large Sonoma County ranches and possessed a lively interest in the whole region. With Sidney V. Smith of San Rafael & San Quentin Railroad fame and Andrew Markham of Sonoma County, he formed a syndicate and entered the successful bid.

Except for Smith's bobtailed connection with the "Bobtail Railroad," none of the three had had any railway experience. Prior to their bid, they had made a definite arrangement among themselves. The 70 per cent interest in the S. F. & N. P. to be purchased they would divide equally. But to prevent control of the road from passing to the Seligmans, who already had 30 per cent by virtue of their deal some years before with Mervyn Donahue and had hoped to repeat it and thus obtain a majority interest, the block would be voted as a unit for five years as determined by preliminary ballot among them.

The Court awarded the San Francisco & North Pacific Railway to Foster, Smith and Markham on March 23, 1893. Foster became president and, to a large extent, continued the staff and policies of Mervyn Donahue. He was, however, a far less social but more demanding boss. Economy became the slogan. Frank Zook, who had been chief engineer ever since he left his conductor's job on the Clay Street Hill Railroad in the '70s, was moved from San Rafael to Tiburon and the post of trainmaster added to his duties. Overtime, which had not yet won recognition at the pay car, became a matter of course. There was grumbling, but times were hard in the '90s and it stopped at that. Once the engineer of Foster's special took advantage of being with the big brass and entered a mild complaint. He had to reach the Tiburon roundhouse at 4 a.m. to oil and shine his engine, run to Ukiah where he had a long lay-over, and often was on the road till midnight. "I've been putting in fully twenty hours a day, Mr. Foster," he concluded. "There's twenty-four hours in the day!" snapped the president and walked away.

To Foster, however, belongs much of the credit for opening up the Russian River country as a vacation land. Informal camping in the forests and two-week rocking-chair sojourns at American plan, pitcher, basin, and thunder-mug resort hotels had long been common. Foster was thinking in terms of summer homes and traffic for the Guerneville Branch where logged out country had left rusty rails. He bought some of the cut-over land, now green and bushy with second growth, and opened the first subdivision, Mirabel Park. The lots were grabbed like rings on a merry-go-round, and he followed it with Camp Vacation, Montesano, Russian River Heights, Rio Nido, and Summer Home Park. He put in "street car" service with an open-air coach hauled up and down the branch by the old "Coffee Grinder" No. 99, both relics of the lumber railroad. Soon hundreds of city families boasted vacation homes on the Russian River, and Guerneville converted itself from a hard-drinking, bullwhacking lumber camp to a village of parasols, mandolins and ice-cream sodas.

The Seligmans and their associates had not been pleased with the tripartite acquisition of Mervyn Donahue's stock. They had counted on securing eventual control of the S. F. & N. P. through further financial advances to the young Colonel, now in his grave. They still wanted it, but it was out of the question while the block endured. So they went to work on Sidney Smith.

The results came to light when Foster called a conference with his two partners prior to the stockholders' meeting set for January 21, 1896 to decide their unit vote on the directorate. Smith merely sent a note that he had decided their agreement was invalid and no longer recognized it. At the annual meeting Foster tendered a vote for the whole block including Smith's shares. Smith also tried to vote them— for himself as director. The Seligman stock was also voted for Smith. His election would give them a majority on the board and leave Foster out on a limb. Plainly the chips were down.

Foster's vote was accepted and Smith brought suit. Judge Seawell, in Superior Court, held the block agreement contrary to public policy and not a true proxy. Sidney Smith, said the Court, was a director. And at the next directors' meeting he appeared and took a seat. President Foster glared and instructed the sergeant-at-arms to give Smith the bum's rush and lock the door. Whereupon Judge Seawell irately announced that Foster was in contempt of court. But the Supreme Court reversed Seawell on the whole affair. Foster had won, but it would be a short-lived victory unless he could think of a fast one, for the block agreement, just upheld, had only another year to go.

A. W. Foster stood in no awe of New York financiers. He had been one himself. He organized the California Northwestern Railway Company, and while he still controlled the destinies of the San Francisco & North Pacific leased it lock, stock and barrel for twenty years to his new corporation! Let the Seligmans capture the whole Board— they couldn't break that lease. The New Yorkers recognized they had been outfoxed and sold their stock to Foster.

Orientation map for Chapter XVII showing the N.P.C. at the time it was taken over by John Martin.

XVII

Narrow Gauge Jinx

THE NORTH PACIFIC COAST, meanwhile, was jogging along in its picturesque, just-a-step-from-the-poorhouse style. James Walker had soon been succeeded as president by John W. Coleman, his general manager. After a couple of years, vice-president William Street replaced him, and three years later, 1896, James Burgess Stetson was president of the N. P. C. None of them could turn it into a money-maker. The logging which had been its prime excuse was now history. In 1885 the subsidiary Northwestern Railroad Company had been incorporated to build eight miles from Duncan's Mill to a new operation at Ingram (now Cazadero), but that was soon cut over.

Commuters still flocked to Marin. The booming suburban towns of Corte Madera, Larkspur (at the Indian shell mound where General Fremont had parleyed with Sutter and Vallejo in '48), Kentfield, Ross, San Anselmo, and Fairfax were all on the narrow gauge. In 1889 the Eastland family built a 1¾-mile spur to Mill Valley and called it the San Francisco, Tamalpais & Bolinas Railroad; it was leased to the N. P. C. with more twice-a-day riders. But no railroad ever got rich on commuters. The narrow gauge still staggered under a load of debt that it could never pay — by 1889 it had only reduced the principal of its indebtedness by $6.05! The stockholders had been wiped out once, ownership had changed again, and the new owners surrendered half their holdings in 1897 to make the picture look a little better.

The Mill Valley & Mount Tamalpais Scenic Railway was opened and soon became famous as the "crookedest railroad in the world." Always a great attraction, this peak from which the whole Bay region could be viewed had been accessible only by foot or horseback. The Mill Valleyans had protested bitterly against profaning the mountain with a railroad—they were to tear their hair in anguish thirty-four years later when the rails were taken up. By that time, Tamalpais Tavern would be world renowned as a hideaway for newlyweds and less orthodox twosomes. Mill Valleyans liked things to stay the way they were. Even the incorporation of the town was put over by the local merchants only through hiring a stooge to jump off the 5:15 ferry and thus delay the commuter vote until the polls were closed.

Physically the N. P. C. changed little. Two or three heavier loco-motives had been added to the roster, but the little engines of the '70s were still in use. No. 9, "M.S. Latham," stood with steam up one night at Cazadero. She was to haul the morning southbound passen-ger, but Austin Creek was running bank high after days of torrential rain. Engineer Briggs and Conductor Brown hashed it over and de-cided to run down to the bridge for a look-see. As the engine slowly started, cyclinder cocks hissing and wood smoke churning into the rain, five others climbed into the cab. Brown rode on the pilot. They stopped short of the bridge, and he walked across it, the swash almost lapping at his heels. Briggs, they had agreed, would stay put unless signalled to come ahead. But as Brown plodded further through the murk, lantern swinging, he heard a terrific crash and ran back. Of neither bridge nor No. 9 was there a trace. Had Briggs taken the bobbing lantern for a highball? Days later, six bodies were recovered, but nothing was seen of the engine until the creek had gone down fifteen feet.

Bill Thomas was master mechanic at the shops. (They spelled it "Sausalito" now.) He eyed the wreck of the 9-spot where they hauled her in, considered some ideas he had toyed with, but fixed her up and renumbered her 17 to take the curse off. The charm failed, however, and she was soon back again, demolished in a collision. Now he decided to try out his experiment, and with Stetson's approval and master boilermaker Jim McAdam's help, he went to work.

When the locomotive returned to service in 1900 as No. 21, "Thomas-Stetson," no one could have recognized the once sleek, silver-domed "M.S. Latham." Thomas had altered her direction, her fuel, her system of making steam, and most of all, her appearance. An occasional ride out on the pilot had suggested better visibility for engineers on the wooded hairpin curves of the N. P. C., so he placed the cab in front over the pony truck. Obviously, this would not be practical with wood or coal fuel, so the 21 was rigged to burn oil. Railroads had been experimenting with fuel oil since its first trial in France thirty years before, but oil burners on American rails were still a rarity. McAdams had built the water tube boiler, slanted for good circulation, with sixty-three three-inch tubes through a corrugated furnace inside the boiler shell. The stack was at the rear. The tender was a flat car with vertical tanks for oil and water, and to make the ensemble slightly more bizarre, a large horizontal drum replaced the steam dome.

Thomas was turned down on his application for a patent — unfortunate for him as his unlikely looking contraption was the granddaddy of all the Southern Pacific's front cab articulated giants. But as for her own performance, she was more or less of a headache. The hoggers and tallowpots all hated her—they felt naked out in front like that. After a few years, her boiler was doing duty in a laundry.

November of 1901 had but a few more hours to live when the blackest, densest tule fog of years rolled in on the Bay and blotted out familiar landmarks as it cued bells, foghorns and whistles to take up their duties. The whaleoil headlights on the Market Street cable cars probed feebly through the dripping mist as a few chilly, belated commuters raced under the invisible Ferry Tower and aboard the *San Rafael* for her 6:15 run to home and dinner.

Among them was Dr. J. S. McCue, a horse doctor in his seventies, who was also Corte Madera poundmaster. Famed as an old stager of the Washoe days and later proprietor of a circus, McCue had commuted on the N. P. C. since its opening. The only good thing he had ever been heard to say about it was that no matter how drunk a man might be when he boarded one of its trains, he was sure to be sober by the time he got off. The old doctor was about frozen and as he crossed the apron, weighed in his mind the relative appeal of a cup of steaming coffee in the grill or a shot of bourbon at the bar. The coffee won. He ducked under the polished slowly-turning main shaft that small boys loved to ride over on their bellies, and turned into the crowded lunch room at the starboard bow. Later he decided he should have chosen the whiskey.

Above, in the *San Rafael's* pilot house, old Captain McKenzie rang for half-speed astern and backed out through the thick tule fog. He made a round turn, as the tide required, halting in the middle of it to let an unseen steamer pass. Foghorns on the Oakland ferries were blasting, the sad bells on the docks bonged and a welter of other sonic landmarks shrieked, wailed and tinkled. Nothing could be seen. The *San Rafael* started on her course ten minutes late, her wheels poking at fourteen turns instead of the usual twenty-two. Off Broadway wharf she safely passed the *Tiburon,* and McKenzie shaped his course for Lombard Street to "catch" that distinctive bell, heard it at 6:36, and headed for Alcatraz, steering by compass and tide calculations.

The fog seemed thicker, if such could be, and there was a very heavy ebb tide. Soon he recognized the *Sausalito's* whistle off his starboard bow. Ordinarily, each would keep to the right of Alcatraz Island, so they would never meet, but a dredger working around Arch Rock had blocked one channel.

Captain McKenzie yanked his whistle cord twice to pass to port; put his helm hard a-starboard. Pilot regulations rigidly forbade the use of passing signals without visibility, but the rule was familiarly ignored, and he was late. Two blasts out of the fog from the *Sausalito* agreed with him. But they sounded uncomfortably close and almost dead ahead. Instantly he rang to stop the engine, sounded three short whistles and rang again full speed astern. The big paddles started splashing again, slowly, in reverse.

Down below, Dr. McCue still sipped his coffee and joshed with George Tredway, the waiter. Suddenly there was a god-awful crash, the ferry's hull splintered open before his eyes, and the *Sausalito's* steel prow smashed into the grill and batted him twenty feet through the door. All hell broke loose, so did most of the passengers' self-control. They smashed windows, panicked up the companion ways and fought madly for life preservers. Behind all the racket — the screams, wails and curses, shattering glass and ghostly chorus of fog-horns outside — they heard the ominous background of endless waters pouring through the breach.

McCue took stock of his personal situation. He couldn't swim. He diagnosed a shattered arm, an ear dangling only by a strip of skin, a wrenched back and assorted minor mutilations. Not much good in a free-for-all, he decided, might as well remain aboard until the ship went down. A vial of horse medicine was in his pocket — it was a strong opiate and he downed enough for a team of Percherons, topping it with a snort of whiskey, for bartender Gus was still on the job in the saloon despite the boiling panic.

Sadly enough, the same could not be said for most of the doomed ship's crew. The officers, at least, kept cool and soon restored some semblance of order. McKenzie and the *Sausalito's* Captain Tribble had immediately ordered their ferries lashed together and boats launched. A few of the deckhands and some male passengers of both boats began to pass women and children from the *San Rafael* which was sinking fast. Soon her starboard rail was under water, then her lights blinked out. Splashing through the greedy waves, men dragged the few remaining women to the upper deck where Bartender Gus now handed matrons across to the *Sausalito* as quick and calm as ever he'd passed a Pisco Punch across the bar. Fireman Grelow had dived into the flooded engine room and managed to "bleed" steam from the boilers — at least there would be no explosion.

Captain McKenzie saw that time had about run out. His passengers were almost off — women and children aboard the other ferry and the men bobbing around in life jackets. He saw Dr. McCue, almost the last to join them, step off the deck. Dick, the baggage truck horse, was still tethered in the cabin. McKenzie cut his rope and drove him out, then jumped for the *Sausalito*. He was just in time. With an almost human sob, the *San Rafael* vanished. Twenty minutes before, she had been a proud but aging steamer.

The *Sausalito's* deck resembled a hospital ward. The fog still resembled a cold puree. No one knew where the tides had led them. But the prolonged whistles and failure of the boats to dock had sent two Red Stack tugs to the rescue. One, the *Sea King,* nosed through the soup just as the last life boat brought more sopping, shivering, cork-jacketed survivors, among them McCue, who was still pepped up with horse pills. Tribble grabbed his megaphone and yelled "where are we?" and from the tug they heard the answer: "Off the Presidio light and heading out to sea!"

Flanked by the two tugs, the *Sausalito* inched along to the haven of her slip and the hysterical cheer that greeted her as she loomed between the pilings showed how the word had spread. An Oakland boat was docking at the other end of the Ferry Building, and from it, President Stetson walked ashore, still unconscious of the tragedy. Seventy-five drowned or missing was the news shouted at him, and the blood drained from his face. He hurried to the N. P. C. office and assumed command — put his captains through the third degree and tried to send the tugs out again with a searching party. The Red Stack people, however, refused to risk another trip. A reckless soul named Tucker finally ventured out in an open launch, but he found no one and almost lost himself.

The next day passed under a burden of suspense and rumor. No one knew just who had been aboard, and many, first feared missing, proved to have taken the California Northwestern ferry. The known dead finally shrunk to Tredway, a William Crandell who, though he had once reached safety, had then lost his life trying to save the waiter; and a four-year-old named Cyrus Waller. Despite tales that he had landed happily on one of the lush pastured islands in the Bay, the carcass of Dick, the freight horse, was sighted drifting out to sea.

With the sinking of the *San Rafael,* the North Pacific Coast itself was almost sunk. Official inquiry found both captains equally responsible, for using passing signals in the fog, but commended their subsequent performance and let them off with trivial penalties. But this did not halt the damage suits for injury and supposed death whose number was growing daily. As for McCue, he suggested that President Stetson bring a check for his idea of a reasonable settlement for his injuries, the doctor to accept it or slice off a presidential ear to match his own loss, as he chose. This sporting offer was ignored, and McCue added his suit to the rest.

Disasters seldom come singly. It was only a few days after the *San Rafael* was lost that the N. P. C. was in the papers again with a train wreck. It was a very embarrassing one indeed. For Stetson had been working on a deal to sell the road; it was still very much in the hush-hush stage, and the smash-up was the special in which he had sent his prospects out to inspect the property. It took the San Francisco press only a matter of hours to ferret out full details, and Stetson and his associates sadly concluded their deal was dead.

XVIII

John Martin Takes Over

IT WAS THE unlucky old Latham private car again. John Martin, promoter of the Bay Counties Power Company, was in the party; Eugene de Sabla, its president, R. R. Colgate, the soap and perfume man; and some brokers that Martin and de Sabla hoped would float bonds to recondition the road if they took it over. Stetson's son-in-law, Chauncey Winslow, was their host. As Mr. de Sabla told the story a few weeks before his death in January, 1956:

"At that time there were few bond houses in San Francisco. We succeeded in getting E. H. Rollins & Sons of Boston and N. W. Harris & Co. of Chicago interested. To show them the necessity of the large outlay for repairs to the roadbed of the railroad from Sausalito to Duncan Mills, and especially from there to Cazadero, we resurrected an old private car of the late Mr. Milton Latham, the founder of the railroad (sic). The car was in A-1 shape, with kitchen, big parlor, and observation platform, etc. Much too big and heavy for the road and especially for the rails from Duncan Mills to Cazadero. They were really nothing but two streaks of rust. The road ran about twenty feet above and along a creek through the most beautiful redwood country. Mr. Colgate, who was associated with me in the majority of my enterprises, was along as well as Mr. Rollins and Doctor Harris, neither as young as they used to be, also Mr. Winslow and several others. We intended to have lunch or early dinner at the Cazadero Inn and had provided not only our own French chef, but also among other things, a fine big turkey which the chef was cooking slowly in the car's galley,

118

or kitchen. Well, about 3 PM, a couple of miles from our destination, the car left the two streaks of rust, although travelling at a snail's pace, and turned over, sending poor Martin, who was standing on the open platform, flying into the upper part of a small redwood tree growing from the bed of the creek about twenty feet below, and from which he was holding on like grim death. Rollins, Doctor Harris and the others, including Colgate found themselves lying on the ceiling, with me on top of Colgate who was yelling 'look out for my glasses and keep your stern out of my face.' This I promptly did, helped the others to their feet, yelled to Martin to be a hero and hold on to his tree and rushed to the galley where the chef was yelling 'bloody murder' as the galley was on fire! He said 'never mind me, my turkey she is burning' etc. By that time the conductor, engineer, etc. of the forward part of the train, which had not been derailed, came running back, so we rescued the turkey, then the chef, and the balance of his treasures. All of which were taken with due ceremony to Cazadero Inn where later on we had a feast that was thoroughly enjoyed by all. We got Martin off his perch in the trees, none the worse for his experience, of which he was very proud, showing his agility."

The cause of the wreck had been obvious. The rail on a sharp curve had been fastened down with bent nails instead of track spikes and they had let go. "Gentlemen," said John Martin to the others, "we'd better buy this railroad and fix it up so folks won't get killed on it."

The new syndicate took over the North Pacific Coast on January 6, 1902, and rechristened it North Shore Railroad forthwith. John Martin announced plans for changing the character of the old line completely. It was to be standard gauged and double-tracked to San Rafael and Mill Valley and first-class trolley trains installed for commuters. Power from the Colgate generators on the Yuba River would run them. The rest of the line from San Anselmo to Cazadero would be put in first-class shape again (no more bent nails) and the White's Hill stretch, where the right-of-way was about to expire anyhow, relocated to avoid the long pull. Two new ferries would be built. "Once more in the checkered career of the North Pacific Coast

Railroad" observed the *Chronicle* "a new set of owners has appeared, ready and anxious to coddle it into a state of prosperity."

Martin and de Sabla, pioneers in long distance high voltage transmission, rushed the face lifting of the narrow gauge. The staff that they assembled later became national leaders in the development of electric traction.

The trolley plan was discarded by Superintendent A. H. Babcock in favor of third rail (really a fourth rail with the concurrent narrow gauge). At Alto, near Mill Valley Junction, the power house was built — here the 60,000-volt three-phase alternating current from Yuba River, 180 miles away, was stepped down to 600 volts direct current. A huge storage battery of 288 large cells, with "juice" enough to run the whole railroad for half an hour, absorbed fluctuations when trains stopped and started, and could carry on in emergencies until the steam stand-by plant took over. Rolling stock was ordered from the St. Louis Car Company and from Pullman — big wide cars to seat sixty-six and equipped with the Hedley trucks which had been perfected on the Chicago els.

The Corte Madera tunnel obviously could not be double-tracked, and Martin installed electric semaphores, newly designed by the Union Switch and Signal Company, for its protection. Since the trains were propelled by direct current, alternating current in the track rails was used to operate the signals. The successful experience with this block installation on the North Shore later led to its adoption on the entire New York subway system.

As the electricification progressed, San Francisco street car motormen applied for jobs by the score, but they were all turned down — the North Shore would use its old steam engineers exclusively.

On the evening of August 19, 1903, electric service was introduced to Mill Valley with a special train of officials and guests. At Sausalito, Engineer Charles Stocker reached for the controller handle instead of a throttle, and the five Tuscan-red, gold striped cars started smoothly. Nine minutes later, he pulled into Mill Valley — running time with steam was an even fifteen. The station was festooned with Japanese lanterns, red fire glowed atop Mount Tamalpais, and the shouts and cheers of the summer crowd mingled with the unfamiliar air horn of the new train.

The little silver-striped Forney 2-spot, known affectionately as "The Jackrabbit," that for years had handled Mill Valley service, was seen no more on the branch. It was the loss of an old friend that the slick new electric could not quite erase. Her whistle had sounded their fire alarms; her bell, cast with silver dollars, called them to the day's chores. She had even been wont to wait in front of their homes and ride them down to the Junction fraternally in her cab.

The electric trains were running to San Rafael in a few more weeks, and steam narrow gauge commuter service was a thing of the past. Now, indeed, the Sausalito five-fifteeners could lord it over the "broad gauge" folks still riding in antique coaches and straining their cinder-filled eyes under oil lamps to read their *Bulletins*. John Martin's electrics were a huge success.

His operation of the narrow gauge main line to Cazadero, however, brought him no glory. The hoodoo persisted, and as always, had it in for specials. Old Warren Dutton passed away about this time, and his dying request was that his old favorite, the "Tomales," pull his family's train to the funeral. The railroad put on No. 4 and said she was the "Tomales" — the names had long been painted over on the cabs, and no one could tell the difference. The special was an hour late getting in, and the Dutton family requested that her departure be similarly postponed. Conductor Burroughs refused, but left two of the three coaches behind for the 3:40 to pick up. The No. 4, actually the old "Olema," thus departed with a single car bearing those anxious to get back to the City. "Shorty" Orth at the throttle was not the most careful engineer in the world, and this was his first run on the North Shore. He had just been fired from the South Pacific Coast for the unpardonable crime of allowing the water in his engine to get low and burning out a crownsheet.

Whipping around a curved trestle south of Point Reyes, the mourner's coach jumped the rails, bumped along the timbers a piece, and then, with the tender, shot into space and landed sliding on its roof, wheels still spinning. No. 4, though derailed, remained on the bridge. The Oakland Congregational Cadets, encamped close by, rushed to the rescue, but they had to send for axes before they could reach those screaming in agony within the twisted car.

Burroughs, badly hurt, blood pouring from a head wound, raced up the track with a red flag the instant he was freed; fainted when he had stopped the following locomotive.

The ensuing hours were a nightmare. Though one of the cadets had rushed to Point Reyes with the news and the regular train was standing there, its conductor refused to move — he had no orders. Finally one of the passengers pulled the pin on the baggage car and persuaded the engineer to start without him — forty or fifty men jumped aboard to help. The Cadets had done an excellent first-aid job, but it was torture for many when they were carried over the dirt road to Point Reyes and an improvised hospital, moved again aboard a relief train which had not arrived for hours, and then slowly jogged homeward. Two had been killed, and many of the injured considered them the lucky ones.

With necessary repairs to the track and unnecessary and never explained official delays, it was 1:30 a.m. when the train of misery crawled into Sausalito. The twenty-five badly injured had suffered ten hours of travail, unfed except for a few sardines and crackers, and racked by the hard seats and jolting progress. A storm of press denunciation followed. It was not mollified when the North Shore's attorney, with rare tact, called the papers to say the railroad was not liable as the passengers had paid no fares but were guests of the Dutton family.

Three days later, No. 20, hauling the up-country train, went off a fill north of Tocaloma. No passengers were hurt, but the hogger was almost killed and the fireman scalded. A rescue train was dispatched to bring them in and through lack of flagging, crashed right into the standing coaches, which kept the narrow gauge in the headlines. Another week, and No. 11 found the Fourth of July crowds too heavy as she tried to haul train 6 back from the River and stalled on the grade near Occidental. No. 3, sent north to help her, banged into the waiting train, breaking the couplers and convincing many of the passengers they'd feel safer in a new-fangled horseless carriage than on the narrow gauge. The crews finally haywired a connection, using the off-set couplers installed by Martin to handle broad-gauge cars, and proceeded. At Point Reyes they broke down again, and a third engine was required to help the tired train get its tired passengers into Sausalito seven hours late. "Mr. Martin," the press and public said, "your electric trains are swell, but for heaven's sake, spare a thought for the old steam narrow gauge."

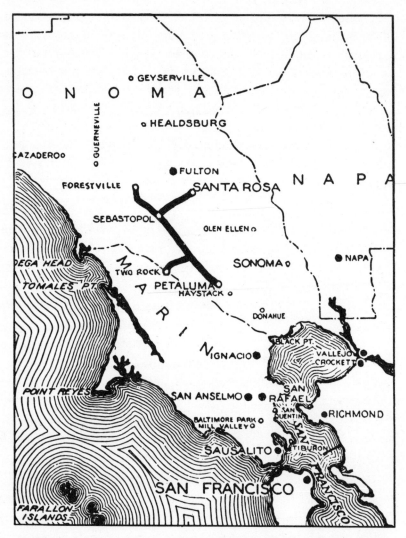

Orientation map for Chapter XIX showing the Petaluma & Santa Rosa electric lines.

XIX

"Juice" Line Challenge

OVER ON THE California Northwestern, A. W. Foster was having his troubles too, but of a different sort. The new electric interurbans were nosing into his Sonoma County preserves. Organized by the Spreckels sugar interest, who were becoming deeply involved in electric traction, and the McNears of Petaluma, supporters of local railroad plans since the days of Charlie Minturn, the Petaluma & Santa Rosa Railway, was chartered June 20, 1903. It would join the title cities with cars greased by lightning. Branches to Forestville and to Bloomfield (which had been promised rails by Harpending, Latham, Stanford, Donahue, and various others, but never did get them) were contemplated. Steamer connections between Petaluma and both sides of the Bay would be a part of the new system. It would cut heavily into the C. N. W. egg and poultry business, its fruit traffic from Sebastopol, and its short haul passenger volume.

In Santa Rosa, three separate horse car systems had cloppity-clopped over rickety rails for years. A family pass good for a month could be had for $1.50 — before the era of baby-sitters it was handy, if folks wanted to step out a while, just to put the kids on the horse car with the family pass pinned on to blouse or pinafore; pick them off later as it ambled by again. These companies, the Central, Union, and Santa Rosa Street Railways, and the Petaluma horse car line as well, were bought by the new corporation for their franchises.

125

Track laying commenced at the river landing in Petaluma in April, 1904, the old "Bully Boy" from the Heald and Guerne Lumber Company pulling the construction train. The rails were mostly laid alongside county roads. In October, the first big yellow trolley car was operated to Sebastopol, and on December 1, 1904, regular service started between Petaluma and the C. N. W. tracks at the outskirts of Santa Rosa. And then trouble started. The P. & S. R. approached the Sonoma County seat from the west; to enter the city it would have to cross the steam road's tracks within the yard limits. A. W. Foster was not having any. If the electric road wished to get across, he said, it could build an overpass or subway. A grade crossing would be a menace to public safety.

Ninety-two Santa Rosa merchants then signed an ultimatum to Foster: Let the P. & S. R. in, or they'd give it every bit of their freight for a year. The C. N. W. president expressed himself as cut to the quick at this lack of loyalty from old friends, but announced he was standing pat. He cut his Sebastopol fare from 30¢ to a dime, 5¢ below the electrics and slashed other competitive rates to match. Then he ordered locomotives Nos. 12 and 13 to be equipped with nozzles capable of shooting live steam in all directions and kept ready in the Santa Rosa yard against any strong-arm tactics.

The P. & S. R. steel was laid to the steam road's tracks and continued on the other side. One night the trolley was stretched across. The Northwestern track foreman eyed it sourly the next morning and slung his steel tape over it to check the clearance. It formed a neat short circuit and he did a very fine impromptu hula until the tape slipped off.

1905 was but three days old when General Manager Alfred Bowen of the electric line accepted Foster's challenge. A built-up cross-over, loaded on a flat car, was shoved up to the intersection. His gang got busy with hack saws on the C. N. W. rails — but not for long. Converging from each end of the yard, No. 12 and No. 13 sprayed a barrage of steam and boiling water to meet head-to-head in grim resemblance to the Last Spike. The P. & S. R. gandy-dancers

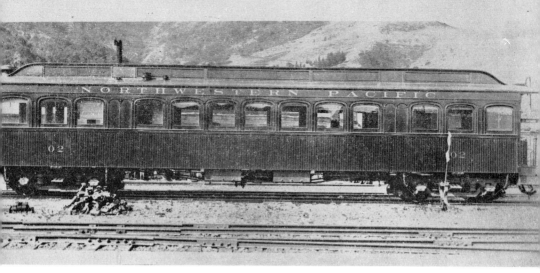

Milton Latham's private car MILLWOOD.

From left to right: E. H. Shoemaker, superintendent North Pacific Coast Railroad, John Martin,
R. R. Colgate, and Eugene de Sabla, Sunday, December 22, 1901. A few hours later their inspection
tour in the MILLWOOD of the N.P.C. came to a sudden, undignified halt.

Eugene de Sabla

North Shore motor ELECTRA was loaned to San Francisco to help clean up debris after the 1906 fire. On the right, monument to Peter Donahue, erected by his son, and still standing at Market, Bush and Battery.

Train No. 9, Engine 92, left Cazadero at 5:55 AM, due in Sausalito 10:03, but the crew had time to visit a bit at "Miller's Retreat."

Engineer W. C. King and Miss Carolyne Rockfort of Point Reyes look at North Shore train. It had been scheduled to leave Point Reyes at 6:10 AM, Wednesday, April 18, 1906. The San Francisco earthquake came at 5:14 AM. King was to have been its engineer.

N.P.C. No. 21, the grand-daddy of the monster S.P. cab-in-front locomotives. Taken at Sausalito in 1900 as the engine neared completion.

N.P.C. No. 21 with a passenger train at Howard's (now Occidental).

H. S. Graham

"The Battle of Sebastopol Avenue," Santa Rosa, March 1, 1905. Note the built-up crossing on the flat car in the right foreground.

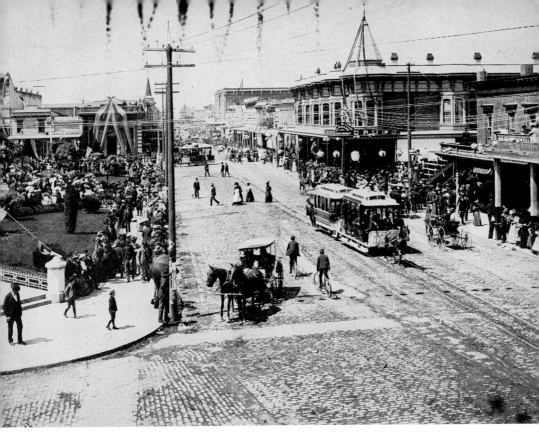

Courthouse Square, Santa Rosa, in the '80s. Before the days of "baby-sitters" the horse-cars served the purpose.

Courthouse Square, Santa Rosa, about 1909. The Petaluma & Santa Rosa electric cars have replaced the horse-cars.

The "Big White Cars" of the Petaluma & Santa Rosa Railroad at Sebastopol, 1909.

A little trouble out on the line. Petaluma & Santa Rosa Railroad.

H. S. Graham

Second No. 8, double-heading, picks up holiday crowds at Monte Rio on the Fourth of July, 1913.

Vacation's Over! Boarding the train at Guernewood Park before the days of sport clothes.

Waiting for the train at Healdsburg on a summer day in 1908. The bus met all trains for the convenience of Hotel Sotoyome guests.

This engine, formerly No. 9 I. E. JAMES of the Virginia & Truckee, with an ex-S. P. tender was working on the Northwestern Pacific construction job near South Fork in 1911 when a slide, harbinger of many more to follow, bowled her over.

N.W.P. Train No. 7 (daily except Sunday) stops at Camp Meeker circa 1910. Rose Hill Hotel on the right.

Finale for the Narrow Gauge. The "boneyard" at Point Reyes in November, 1931.

Roy D. Graves

Furthest northwest advance of the Santa Fe cross. Eureka depot circa 1904 with S.F. & N.W. No. 3 (ex E.R.&E. No. 3 DEFENDER) with the train for Alton.

Island Mountain. One example of the heavy construction involved in building a railroad through the Eel River Canyon.

Arthur L. Lloyd

Wallace Sorrel

Progress in commuting. A train of ex-narrow-gauge coaches rebuilt into standard gauge electrics by John Martin's North Shore at "B" Street, San Rafael in 1904. (Compare with picture facing page 15.)

One of the big Aluminum interurban cars with which the N.W.P. commute service was partially modernized in the '20s. The photo was taken at San Anselmo from almost the exact spot as picture facing page 31.

Addison Laflin

The Mt. Tamalpais & Muir Woods Railway train starts to back up the mountain after passengers have changed from the Northwestern Pacific electric cars at Mill Valley.

One of the cars built by the St. Louis Car Company in 1902 for the North Shore electrification.

A Northwestern Pacific electric train near Escalle in 1938. These cars were formerly narrow-gauge coaches.

Interior of North Shore electric car.

The Gold Spike Special ready to pull out of Sausalito early on the morning of October 23, 1914. After the spike-driving ceremonies at Cain Rock it went on to become the first through train to Eureka. Electric commuter trains on the left.

Northwestern Pacific president W. S. Palmer wields a silver spike maul as his daughter Alice steadies
the gold spike that finally linked San Francisco and Eureka by rail at Cain Rock, October 23, 1914.
Two rows behind Alice stands "Sunny Jim" Rolph, usually out in front.

Since the first printing of this book, two prominent rail historians, Mr. Roy Graves and Mr. Walter Howe have identified the men in this picture. Paul Helmore (right) was Chief Clerk and later became Justice of the Peace in Sausalito. David Parsley is the Engineer.

N.W.P. No. 21 proudly pulls train No. 1 at Preston in 1908. The train left Sherwood
at 11:15 AM; due in Tiburon 7:00 PM.

N.W.P. No. 201 with mixed train No. 534 at Sherwood in 1908. Northern terminus soon to be
orphaned when the final location to Eureka was chosen.

The boys at Tiburon were pretty proud of this new switcher when she arrived from the American Locomotive Works around Christmas in 1910.

Just before the Depression the Northwestern Pacific passenger power sported a two-tone green livery with redwood tree herald on the tender that was as handsome as any ever worn by the iron horse.

Dave Joslyn

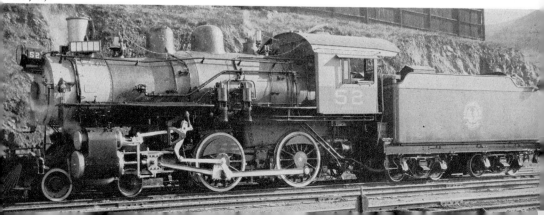

A familiar sight to the homeward-bound N.W.P. commuter—the Sausalito ferry slips. The boats are the *Ukiah* and *Sausalito*.

Fort Seward. When the railroad came through a town was laid out and a fine station and large hotel erected—then the whole townsite was sold for a farm.

leapt for their lives, and only an innocent by-standing nickelodeon ticket-taker was badly scalded.

In dejected defeat, Bowen's men retired and the crossover was hauled away. The locomotives also returned to the sidelines for fuel and water. A little later the trolley car "Woodworth" ran down to the end of track. This occasioned no suspicion as it had been operating from that point to Sebastopol. But suddenly things began to happen in a hurry. Out of the "Woodworth" poured the P. & S. R. track gang; they seized ties already stacked there for the job and threw them across the Northwestern track on both sides. Several spans of mules and horses also appeared out of nowhere. They were hurriedly hitched to the "Woodworth," and the trolley was hauled bumpety-bump across the tracks and onto its own rails on the other side before the locomotive crews could breach the barriers of ties and bring their steam-snorting behemoths into play.

It was a battle won by the electric line, but the war was far from over. Another track had to be crossed, a brewery spur, and the next day Foster secured a temporary injunction against cutting either one. The "Woodworth" was marooned between the Northwestern main line and the spur, and Bowen's plan to use her in shuttle service up to town, with passengers walking across the C. N. W. tracks to the other cars, until he could effect a track crossing was stymied. However, the merchants provided an omnibus service at their own cost to connect with the electric cars.

Two months later, on listening to the arguments of both sides, Judge Seawell dissolved his injunction and on March 1st the battle was joined again at an even more desperate pitch.

Early in the morning the P. & S. R. freight train arrived at the scene with the cross-over and a small army of workmen, armed with picks and shovels and under the command of Superintendent Fairchild. Foster's forces were ready and waiting. His mobile artillery, Nos. 12 and 13, were popping their safety valves and he had cars loaded with earth and men with shovels. At a signal from Fairchild the electric men began to dig an excavation for the crossing. Simultaneously the steam men shovelled earth from their flat cars back into the hole. Some of it fell on the heads and shoulders of the toiling P. & S. R. crew and Fairchild had trouble to keep his men swinging their picks at the ground instead of at their tormentors. Then the two locomotives entered the fray belching steam and routing their opponents. But as soon as the valves were closed those who were not scalded went to work again, and then there was more steam to stop them.

The scene developed into a first-class Donnybrook and it is a miracle there were no serious casualties. Curses and threats were shouted and rocks flew through the air. To add to the tumult the trolley wire fell, spitting sparks, but somehow no one was electrocuted. Fairchild's men managed to drive two wagons onto the steam road's tracks while the engines were backed away but this attempt to keep the area clear also failed as the locomotives merely returned and smashed the wagons to kindling.

Shortly after noon two more Northwestern engines arrived with additional cars of earth and reinforcements from the Petaluma section gang. As news of the warfare spread a crowd of some 3,000 gathered, mostly rooting for the electric cars. As the battle reached its highest pitch and the steam-spouting locomotives bore down once more on the weary P. & S. R. crew the horrified crowd gasped to see Director F. A. Bush fling himself on the track in the path of one of the approaching engines. It ground to a sudden halt, just short of him by inches.

The steam men tried to break his grip on the rails, the electric men tried to rescue him from his attackers, and between them poor Bush was, for several minutes, the wherewithal of a tug-of-war. At this point Chief Severson and a squad of Santa Rosa police arrived in the paddy-wagon. The Chief demanded that the C. N. W. leaders desist from obstructing the work on the crossing. Being less afraid of the consequences of ignoring the Santa Rosa police than disobeying Foster, Chief Engineer Zook and other Northwestern men were taken to court in the wagon. The battle, however, continued.

About four o'clock mutual exhaustion forced a kind of truce. Also word went around that the P. & S. R. people had applied to the Superior Court in San Francisco for a restraining order against the Northwestern. Shortly after five President Foster himself pulled in from San Rafael on a special train with 150 reinforcements. But just as he stepped off his business car a telegram was handed to him that Judge Hunt had granted the restraining order. Foster took it like a man. He called off his army and his engines and said the Court order would be respected.

The electric men, however, took no chances. They strung lights overhead and work went on into the night until the crossing was completed. It was well after midnight when tired cheers greeted the first electric car to rattle over the C. N. W. crossing and proceed on up to Courthouse Square. The Battle of Sebastopol Avenue was history.

The Petaluma & Santa Rosa Railway did cut heavily into the Northwestern's revenues. It was popular, fast, and frequent. The big yellow interurbans with their open trailers, trolley wheels spitting sparks, were the fad for picnics and excursions. For years it was a further threat as extensions were proposed — to Dillon's Beach, to Camp Meeker, to Guerneville, Clear Lake and Healdsburg, or south to McNear's Point with frequent ferries to the City. But these never got past the paper stage.

XX

Giants Battle to a Draw

THE CALIFORNIA NORTHWESTERN, and the North Shore as well, had now again come within the orbit of the giants. The Big Four lay in their sarcophagi; the Southern Pacific in the firm, ambitious hands of E. H. Harriman. The Santa Fe, by purchase of the Valley Road and the California & Nevada had now reached Oakland, and its president, Edward Payson Ripley, had set no limits on its aspirations either. Both had their eyes upon Eureka, the redwood traffic, and possibly coastal Oregon beyond.

The Eurekans had almost abandoned hope of ever seeing a through train to San Francisco. One brilliant scheme after another had fallen flat. In 1890, there had been a flurry. A visiting S. P. official had talked big to the local press about an impending line from the end of the Vaca Valley branch through Lake County and down the Eel River canyon. It proved to be all talk. A local banker announced he'd head a "People's Railroad" south. The banker went off to Alaska, and the people continued to ride the Idaho Stage Company between Hydesville and Ukiah. Feelers came from Red Bluff for joint efforts toward a connecting railway. Cooperation was gladly offered, but the Red Bluffers were bluffing.

But now, in 1903, mansard filagree Eureka felt like an old maid suddenly besiged by two wealthy swains on bended knees. Very quietly, Santa Fe agents had acquired the Eel River & Eureka, on which the S. P. once had held an option. They had sewed up The

Pacific Lumber Company's road up the Eel past Scotia to Shively, the California Midland just built from Hydesville to Carlotta, and the California & Northern, running north from Eureka along the bay to Arcata. They had also tied up large virgin tracts of timberland.

Then Ripley approached A. W. Foster about the California Northwestern and its lease of the S. F. & N. P., but Ed Harriman had been there first with a cash offer. Foster had not accepted; he had promised an answer within ninety days and considered himself verbally committed to the S. P. if he sold at all, although Ripley offered a half a million more. After considerable cogitation, the broker decided he had had enough of railroading and accepted Harriman's proposition.

Harriman had not overlooked the North Shore Railroad. He didn't believe the Santa Fe could use it in a Eureka line, but it had nuisance value. As for Martin, he was ready to get out. He had concluded there was more profit selling electricity than running railroads, and he was deeply concerned by operating troubles at White's Hill. After the electrification his prime project for improving the road had been a new tunnel at a lower elevation to replace the old meandering route. The farmers, however, had asked outrageous prices for a new right-of-way. The Burdells, to the west, on the contrary, had offered a pathway free. So Martin had shifted the railroad to the other side of the valley, opening the new tunnel December 4, 1904, and the disgruntled farmers on the east were left without any railroad — high or low. Strange things began to happen — unexplainable derailments, dead cows tied to the track, vague rumors of worse to follow. Martin told his family he just couldn't risk having innocent people killed by the personal antagonism of these die-hards toward himself.

So Martin went to New York and called on Harriman. He and de Sabla owned all the North Shore stock, he said, and they thought Harriman might be interested in taking it off their hands in connection with his California Northwestern purchase. Harriman listened and invited Martin to lunch; over coffee informed him that he was not interested in buying their stock.

"We are not asking you to buy it, we are giving it to you!" was Martin's reply, as de Sabla relates the story: "This was too much for E. H. and he said 'All right, I'll take it, there must be a Santa Claus around.' Two or three months later Martin received a check for $100,000 to be divided between Martin and myself. Very fine of him! Naturally when it was known that Harriman, or the Southern Pacific, owned the stock, the price of the bonds went well over par, and in demand, so I made a very substantial profit and I assume Martin and Colgate did likewise."

Foster, at Harriman's request, took charge of both roads. He was through with the railroad business though, he said — this was only a temporary accommodation, and he would accept no salary for it.

Disappointed in not snaring the old Donahue Line, which Foster had by now extended from Ukiah to Willits as the San Francisco & Eureka Railroad and was pushing on to Sherwood, Ripley consoled himself that he had Humboldt County tied up beyond any Harriman threat. He organized the San Francisco & Northwestern Railway Company to combine the Eel River & Eureka and the other roads, with Captain A. H. Payson, president. Up on the tower of Eureka station went the Santa Fe cross. And survey parties rushed a line up the south fork of the Eel and through Lake, Napa and Solano Counties to the Santa Fe main line. Ripley also got the forty-mile Albion & Southeastern, a lumber road from Albion on the coast to Christine, renamed it Fort Bragg & Southeastern, and planned to extend it up the Navarro River, through Healdsburg to a junction with the other line. All this, he felt, should squelch Mr. Harriman pretty completely.

Complacency could be expensive when the "Boy Wonder of Wall Street" was on the other team, as Ripley should well have known. He struck a derail when Harriman announced an agreement with lumber tycoon A. B. Hammond for his railroads, the Eureka & Klamath River north to Trinidad, the Corvallis & Eastern and the Astoria & Columbia River. Together these lines covered almost 300 miles. Hammond had envisioned combining them into a Eureka-Portland railroad. The Southern Pacific could go ahead with this plan, and the Santa Fe would have to stop drooling over dreams of a redwood monopoly. To make matters more uncomfortable for Ripley, the Eureka & Klamath River even had some claims to trackage rights over the Eel River & Eureka.

The two rajahs of the rails had pretty effectually outfoxed each other. Neither wanted to spend $150,000 a mile building all the lines they talked about so casually. Both knew from careful extensive research that two railroads to Eureka, with the terrific heavy construction costs involved, would only starve each other. But neither knew much about backing down, and neither built a foot of track for three years for fear of starting the other off to the races. Finally, somehow, they got together. Perhaps the fact that agents of Gould's new Western Pacific were snooping around played a part. At last a railroad was really coming through Beckwourth Pass and, until it secured a Sacramento franchise, seemed likely to head through Lake County and Marin. On November 24, 1906, Harriman and Ripley formed the Northwestern Pacific Railway Company as a temporary instrument of compromise.

Within this framework, their henchmen negotiated a concordat and attacked the physical problem. It resolved itself, after all, merely to connect Sherwood and Shively with a hundred miles of railroad, but through a rugged mountain wilderness notable for torrential rainfall and almost complete absence of wagon roads. Articles of Consolidation were drawn to include all the various railroad properties concerned, and the Northwestern Pacific Railroad was chartered January 8, 1907, its stock evenly divided between Southern Pacific and Santa Fe. Captain Payson was president and James Agler of the S. P. general manager. Of the nine directors each road would appoint four and choose the odd one every other year.

Reconciliation of the recent rivals' construction plans was a more concrete problem. The Southern Pacific had discarded the surveys of Donahue and Foster. It had decided to orphan the Sherwood extension and build down Outlet Creek from Willits to the main Eel River. Santa Fe engineers preferred the original line from Sherwood along the South Fork of the Eel. The final decision was made by a panel of the most high-powered railway engineering talent in the land: William Hood, S. P. Chief Engineer; William Storey, then occupying the same position with Santa Fe; William Edes of the new N. W. P., and a staff of bridge engineers, geologists, and various assorted experts. The whole brigade spent weary weeks in the saddle, equipment packed on mules, exploring every nook and cranny of the two valleys. On emerging from the brush, the three "Bills" agreed that Harriman was right — the main Eel River canyon was the better route.

Work was started at Willits in October but ground to a halt three months later along with most of the nation's activities in the panic of 1907. Almost two years went by while prosperity lingered around the corner, and then construction was resumed in earnest from both ends and several beachheads along the way. Six locomotives from Tiburon took an ocean voyage to Eureka to join those of contractors Willett and Burr on the heavy work south of Shively. This went slowly — twenty-five or thirty miles a year was about all that could be chalked up in this brutal, inaccessible terrain. There were thirty tunnels in the hundred miles, and the geology was so unstable that they were apt to fault out of alignment as soon as they were bored. On much of the job even teams could not get in — hand mucking had to do it all. Winter downpours were not only a constant threat of slides and eroded fill, but often raised the Eel thirty feet overnight. Stranded driftwood high on the bare rocks in the canyon warned the railroaders to keep their elevation. The scenery was gorgeous but mostly unappreciated.

Warren S. Palmer, general superintendent of the Southern Pacific, with an excellent background in engineering and operating, soon succeeded Agler as general manager and then Payson as president. On October 23, 1914, he stood with a silver spike maul between the engine pilots of "Sequoia Specials" from north and south at Cain Rock. His pretty daughter, Alice, held a spike fashioned of Trinity

River gold; the last tie of polished birdseye redwood was in place. Around him stood Mayor Clark of Eureka, San Francisco's "Sunny Jim" Rolph, officials of Southern Pacific and Santa Fe, and others lucky enough to wangle invitations. Palmer pounded in the spike and then Alice shattered a bottle of California champagne on the rail.

The last spike was driven. But the long awaited train from San Francisco was not to reach Eureka on the red letter day. For while the little gathering at Cain Rock gave its attention to spike and speeches, tumbling boulders were burying the railroad thirty miles up the line. The "Sequoia Specials," like many a regular train to follow, had to wait while the track was dug out. The planned celebration in Eureka waited too, until they finally pulled in at 3 a.m. The Eurekans, having waited half a century, did not weaken at a few hours more. The grand parade was held in the small hours of the morning.

Now, at last Asbury Harpending's dream of the San Francisco & Humboldt Bay Railroad was realized. Back in California for the first time since the famous diamond hoax and at seventy-five still making fortunes — and losing them — he paused to speculate on what might have been had he hung on to his railroad instead of pleasing Ralston. Of the old-timers, he was almost the sole survivor. John Romer, who had helped him, died the day the spike was driven.

Though steel finally linked the two seaports the new roadbed was in no condition for regular service, particularly with the rains about to start. It was on July 1, 1915, that scheduled service was begun from Sausalito to Trinidad.

On the later history of the Northwestern Pacific Railroad, it is the intention of this account to dwell but briefly. The diverse railways which went into its birth, Warren Palmer integrated into an efficient system. Alternating control did not ease his job as both Santa Fe and S. P. seemed to use their biennial reigns mainly as a means of dumping antique rolling stock. The Union Lumber Company's California Western, opened from Fort Bragg to Willits in 1912, removed all excuse to link Albion with Healdsburg, though the dotted "proposed" line to the orphan branch remained on N. W. P. maps for years.

Constant effort was made by the Lake County leaders to secure a branch from Hopland, but they never did.

Standard gauge was extended from Guerneville to Duncan's Mills, and for years the "Triangle Trip" — north via Santa Rosa and Fulton to Monte Rio, return by narrow gauge — was one of California's most popular excursions. Picnic crowds were easier on the rolling stock now, though the decibels from a trainload bawling "Everybody's Doing It!" to some garlic-scented Sicilian's accordion pumping matched those of the earlier days. On summer holidays all freights were annulled and engines and crews put on special passenger runs. All trains had two locomotives—sometimes three or four—and ran in sections. Twenty-five or thirty coaches would be borrowed from the S. P., along with a ferry or two, and it was not uncommon for 100,000 merrymakers to pour through the Sausalito mole on a single summer day. Northwestern Pacific meant "fun" to thousands. Its annual *Vacation,* describing the resorts it served, was almost an inch thick and eagerly watched for every year.

John Martin's third-rail Suburban System, its dark red cars now painted Pullman green, handled the ever-growing commuter traffic for thirty-eight years — safely and efficiently. In 1929, some steel and aluminum cars, similar to the S. P. East Bay equipment were added. Pumpkin-colored, they revived the old livery of the San Rafael & San Quentin, though probably sentiment had little to do with the decision.

With the merger, Tiburon had been discontinued as a passenger terminal. The old Donahue line was linked with Sausalito by a connection at Baltimore Park.

The main line, with its day and night trains each way, Pullmans on the latter to Eureka and Fort Bragg, barely paid fixed charges on the huge investment. Maintenance in the land of eighty-inch rains and ever-restless geology was a man-size problem, and it was a rare winter that the road wasn't shut down for a few days or weeks. One slide, hundreds of feet wide and a mile high, took $50,000 worth of drains to lick. Another is still sliding all the time, and the track gangs watch it like hawks.

In 1929, Southern Pacific bought out the Santa Fe and assumed sole ownership of the road. The first result was immediate death for the narrow gauge. Since 1920, the little trains had only run between Point Reyes and the Russian River. Now they were hauled into the yard and sold to the Japanese for scrap. With the growing use of the highway and the depression, the railroad that once took in more than half its income selling tickets saw one "last train" after another. On July 31, 1933, such a one steamed slowly out of Point Reyes and up Paper Mill Creek, bell tolling as the whole town watched and many cried. November 14, 1935, saw engineer Bill Burns, who had run the first train into Duncan's Mills, at the throttle as Train 202 unbelievably wound up the Russian River service. There was another picnic in honor of the event, but not a joyous one. The Sonoma Valley service, the trains to Trinidad, the day express to Eureka, all soon followed, though of course these rails were kept for freight. In 1932, the Petaluma & Santa Rosa Railway sold out to Northwestern Pacific, and passenger service on the electric line was abandoned. Then, because of the new Golden Gate Bridge, John Martin's fine interurban system was junked on February 28, 1941. Marin commuters henceforth could ride buses.

The daylight Eureka trains, numbers 1 and 2, were discontinued on May 10, 1942. From that date until June 2, 1956 the only passenger service was the overnight express. Leaving San Rafael, which had been made the southern passenger terminal with the abandonment of the ferry service, about eight o'clock in the evening, they made the 257 miles to Eureka in a little over twelve hours. The southbound trip was made on a similar schedule. The passengers, of course, had little chance on these night runs to see the impressive scenery through the redwoods and along the Eel River canyon.

These trains did a good business through the war years but patronage sank to almost nothing afterward. Application was made to the Public Utilities Commission for permission to abandon passenger service entirely on the Northwestern Pacific, except for an isolated stretch in the Eel River canyon where there were no highways, but the Commission refused to allow this and ordered a triweekly daytime service between San Rafael and Eureka.

Accordingly, a new train named "The Redwood" was inaugurated with some fanfare on June 2, 1956. A small train, it is nevertheless streamlined and air-conditioned and although it has not been in service long enough at this writing to speculate on its eventual fate, it has won considerable public popularity because of its pleasant scenic ride.

"The Redwood" runs up to Eureka on Mondays, Thursdays and Saturdays; returns to San Rafael on the days following—about what Harpending might have managed in the way of passenger service had he finished his road to Eureka in 1869. It averages about 25 miles per hour, which is probably a little better than Harpending could have done with the woodburners then available. But even Harpending, to whom nothing looked impossible, would be amazed at the long freight trains that come down from the redwood country.

Northwestern Pacific today is a busy, efficient freight hauler. Well maintained, completely dieselized, it is a valuable subsidiary of the Southern Pacific. Talk with its train crews though, and you will find a few old-timers who remember their pride in the many busy, bustling passenger trains of years ago; who still hope, somehow, to see more "varnish" on the line again. They still have the redwoods, but they miss the picnics and the commuters.

Appendices

THE LOCOMOTIVES OF THE NORTHWESTERN PACIFIC
AND PREDECESSOR LINES

This roster is included in order that the reader may trace the origin and disposition of specific locomotives. Limitations of space prevented the inclusion of data on cars, electric and otherwise.

Here is a brief explanation of the condensed descriptive system used. The number after the builders name is the factory serial number and is important in following the carrier of an often sold locomotive. The column headed "Type" refers to wheel arrangement, the first figure being the number of wheels in the pony truck, second, the number of drivers, and third, the number of trailing wheels. A following letter "T" indicates an engine with the water tank attached, there being no separate tender for this type. "Cylinders" give in inches the bore (diameter) of the cylinder and the piston stroke. "Drivers" gives the diameter in inches of the drivers, or large wheels.

139

NORTH PACIFIC COAST (Narrow Gauge)

No.	Name	Built	Builder	Type	Cylinders	Drivers	Remarks	NWP No.
1	Saucelito	1874	Baldwin (3495)	4-4-0	12x16	40	Sold to L. E. White Lumber Co., Elk, Calif.	89
2	San Rafael	1874	Mason (537)	0-4-4F	12x16	44	Scrapped 1911	—
3	Tomales	1875	Baldwin (3722)	4-4-0	12x16	42	Scrapped 1913	83
4	Olema	1874	Baldwin (3629)	4-4-0	12x16	42	Scrapped 1908	81
5	Bodega	1875	Baldwin (3703)	4-4-0	12x16	42	Scrapped 1899, parts used in NS #21	—
6	Valley Ford	1874	Baldwin (3664)	4-4-0	12x16	42	Lsd. to Dollar Lbr. Co., '99-'01, renumbered 22	22
7	Tamalpais	1875	Baldwin (3721)	4-4-0	12x16	42	Scrapped 1908	80
8	Bully Boy	1877	Mason (584)	0-6-6F	13x17	38	Scrapped 1911	88
9	M. S. Latham	1875	Baldwin (3749)	4-4-0	12x16	42	Wrecked 2/14/94, rebuilt as No. 17	—
10	Bloomfield	1877	Baldwin (3840)	4-4-0	12x16	42	Sold '95 to Ferrocarril Occ. de Guatemala (#51)	—
11	Marin	1878	Baldwin (3842)	4-4-0	12x16	42	Scrapped 1911	82
12	Sonoma	1876	Baldwin (3843)	4-4-0	12x16	42	Sold '79 to Nev. Cent. Ry. (#5), pres. by R&LHS	—
	Tyrone	1877	Baldwin	T	10x14	38		
13		1883	Baldwin (6611)	2-6-0	14x18	39	No. 3 D&RG bought by NPC '88, scrapped '10	195
14		1891	Brooks (1885)	4-4-0	16x20	48	Sold for scrap 1934	92
15		1891	Brooks (1886)	4-4-0	15x20	48	Scrapped 1935	90
16		1894	Brooks (2421)	4-4-0	15x20	48	Sold for scrap 1934	91
17(9)							See No. 9	
18		1899	Brooks (3418)	4-6-0	16x22	55	Scrapped 1935	95
20		1900	N.P.C. (1)	4-4-0	13x18	47	Retired 1920	84
21	Thomas-Stetson	1901	N.P.C. (2)	4-4-0	13x18	47	Scrapped 1905	
22(6)							See No. 6	

ADDITIONAL ENGINES ACQUIRED BY NORTH SHORE

No.	Built	Builder	Type	Cylinders	Drivers	Remarks	NWP No.
10	1880	Baldwin (4960)	4-4-0	14x18	49	#10 SPC, acq. 1907, scrapped 1917	87
17	1884	Baldwin (7249)	4-4-0	14x18	52	#14 SPC, acq. 1907, sold for scrap 1934	93
19	1884	Baldwin (7236)	4-4-0	14x18	52	#15 SPC, acq. 1907, scrapped 1926	86
31	1885	Baldwin (7676)	2-8-0	16x20	37	#20 SPC, purchased 1903 from DSS&A (#31) H&C (#3) "Oscelo"	322
33	1885	Baldwin (7677)	2-8-0	16x20	37	Purch. 1903 from DSS&A (#33) H&C (#2) "Tamarack", scrapped 1915	323
40	1880	Baldwin (4974)	2-8-0	15x18	36	Purch. from D&RG (#44) "Texas Creek"	321

Electra (Std. Gauge)   Electric Motor   Sold to U.R.R., to Pac. Elec. Ry., now at Traveltown

SAN FRANCISCO & NORTH PACIFIC RAILROAD

No.	Name	Built	Builder	Type	Cylinders	Drivers	Remarks	NWP No.
1	San José	1862	Norris (1009)	4-4-0	13x22	57	Formerly S.F. & S.J. #1, Retired 7/15/1920	4
2	J. G. Downey	1870	Union Iron Wks. (14)	4-4-0	14x22	64	Scrapped 7/31/15	6
3	W. J. Ralston	1870	Union Iron Wks. (15)	4-4-0	14x24	64	Retired 4/17/20 (2nd)	7
4	Geyser	1873	Union Iron Wks. (16)	4-4-0	14x24	64	Scrapped 1904	—
5	Santa Rosa	1873	Union Iron Wks. (17)	4-4-0	14x22	63	Scrapped 1911	5
6	Cloverdale	1878	Grant	4-4-0	16x24	63	Scrapped 5/15/12	11
7	Petaluma	1878	Grant	4-4-0	16x24	63	Retired 11/11/26; used in "The Iron Horse"	12
8	San Rafael	1881	Baldwin (5485)	4-4-0	15x24	63	Retired 5/1/25; used in "The Iron Horse"	8
9	Marin	1883	Grant (1664)	4-4-0	16x24	59	Converted to stationary boiler 5/15/38	9
10	Healdsburg	1883	Grant (1665)	4-4-0	16x24	59	Scrapped 6/10/37	10
11	Ukiah	1882	Union Iron Wks. (30)	4-4-0	18x24	60	Scrapped 8/18/07	—
12	Peter Donahue	1884	Rogers (3305)	4-4-0	18x24	61	Scrapped 7/13/37	19
13	Tom Rogers	1884	Rogers (3306)	4-4-0	18x24	61	Scrapped 9/26/36	20
14	Tiburon	1888	Grant	4-4-0	16x24	62	Scrapped 9/26/36	14
15	Eureka	1888	Grant	4-6-0	18x24	55	Retired 5/31/29	102
16	Vichy	1889	Rogers (4154)	4-4-0	17x24	63	Destroyed in wreck near Ignacio 8/8/10	18
17	Lytton	1889	Rogers (4155)	4-4-0	17x24	63	Scrapped 9/21/35	17
18	Skaggs	1889	Rogers (4212)	4-6-0	16x24	57	Retired 9/30/28	101
19		1900	Baldwin (17759)	4-6-0	19x26	57	Scrapped 4/10/37	110
20		1901	Richmond (3304)	4-6-0	18x24	57	Scrapped 12/15/35	103
21		1902	American (25620)	4-6-0	19x26	57	Scrapped 7/17/34	105
22		1904	Baldwin (23933)	4-6-0	19x26	57	Scrapped 4/10/37	107
23		1904	Baldwin (23951)	4-6-0	19x26	57	Scrapped 10/21/48	108
24		1904	Baldwin (24035)	4-4-0	18x24	69	Scrapped 6/10/37	21
25		1902	American (25621)	4-6-0	19x26	57	Scrapped 3/10/34	106
99	"Coffee Grinder"	1887	E. Jardini	0-4-0T	6x10		Sold to North Bend Lumber Co. 2/18/10	99
131	Greyhound	1868	Rhode Island (76)	4-4-0	15x22	56	Purch. from Cen. Pac. 1872, scrapped before 1892	—
132	Deerhound	1868	Rhode Island (77)	4-4-0	15x22	56	Purch. from Cen. Pac. 1872, returned to C.P.	—

ADDITIONAL ENGINES ACQUIRED BY CALIFORNIA NORTHWESTERN RY.

No.	Name	Built	Builder	Type	Cylinders	Drivers	Remarks	NWP No.
30		1900	Baldwin (18179)	4-6-0	19x26	57	Also bore the number 1; scrapped 10/14/48	109
31		1901	Richmond (3303)	4-6-0	18x24	57	Scrapped 9/26/36	104
32		1904	Lima (909)	Shay	13½x15	40	Form. Northwestern Lumber Co. No. 1, sold to Mason, Walsh, Atkinson & Kerr 1/1/35	251
33		1903	Baldwin (22446)	2-6-2T	17x22	47	Retired 10/21/30	201
34		1903	Baldwin (22474)	2-6-2T	17x22	47	Sold for scrap 10/31/37	202

EEL RIVER & EUREKA

No.	Name	Built	Builder	Type	Cylinders	Drivers	Remarks	NWP No.
1	Eel River	1884	Baldwin (7013)	4-4-0	13x22	50	Retired 7/15/20	2
2	Eureka	1884	Baldwin (7400)	4-4-0	13x22	49	Retired 12/4/16	1
3	Defender	1887	Baldwin (8776)	2-6-0	13x22	39	Scrapped 9/20/16	3-151-351
4		1880	Penn. R.R. (1031)	2-6-0	17x24	59	Retired 10/21/30	16
5		1886	Baldwin (8092)	2-6-0	17x24	55	Retired 5/31/29	152-352
							Ex. AT&SF 0179, orig. GC&SF	

EUREKA & KLAMATH RIVER

No.	Name	Built	Builder	Type	Cylinders	Drivers	Remarks	NWP No.
1	Advance	1875	Baldwin (3751)	0-6-0				
2	Gypsy			0-4-0T	8x12	34		
3	Onward	1883	Baldwin (6711)	2-6-0	11x18	36		
4	Challenge	1896	Baldwin (14738)	2-6-0	13x18	42		
5	Patawok	1897	Baldwin (15283)	2-6-0	13x18	42		
6		1887	Baldwin (8947)	4-4-0	14x24	56	Ex. LA & Pacif. No. 3. Orig. L.A. Co. No. 3 (2nd)	3

ADDITIONAL ENGINES ACQUIRED BY OREGON & EUREKA

No.	Name	Built	Builder	Type	Cylinders	Drivers	Remarks	NWP No.
7			Pittsburg	4-4-0	18x26	55	Acquired from Hicks	
8			Grant	2-6-0	20x24	60	Acq. fr. Hicks '02, to Hammond & Little Riv. (#8)	
9			Grant	2-6-0	18x24	50	Acq. fr. Hicks '02, to Hammond & Little Riv. (#9)	
10			Cooke (1720)	4-4-0			Ex. Ore. Pac. #7, Acq. 1898, sold to Rogue River Valley 1905 (#3)	
11			Hammond Shops	2-8-0	19x26	50	To Hammond & Little River (#11)	

PETALUMA & HAYSTACK

No.	Name	Built	Builder	Type	Cylinders	Drivers	Remarks	NWP No.
		1864	Atlas Foundry				Blew up at Petaluma August 27, 1866	—

SAN RAFAEL & SAN QUENTIN

No.	Name	Built	Builder	Type	Cylinders	Drivers	Remarks	NWP No.
	San Rafael	1869	Built in S.F.				Cost $10,367.88, scrapped at Saucelito 1875	—
	"Dummy"	1870						

SONOMA VALLEY PRISMOIDAL RY.

No.	Name	Built	Builder	Type	Cylinders	Drivers	Remarks	NWP No.
		1876	Pacific Iron Foundry	Prismoidal			Set up as stationary engine at Shellville 1878	—

SONOMA VALLEY RAILROAD

No.	Name	Built	Builder	Type	Cylinders	Drivers	Remarks	NWP No.
1	Sonoma	1878	Baldwin (4455)	0-4-2				—
2	Newton Booth	1879	Baldwin (4583)	4-4-0	10x16	42	Sold to Oahu Ry. & Land Co. (No. 8) 1889	—
3	General Vallejo	1881	Baldwin (5488)	4-4-0			Sold to Oahu Ry. & Land Co. (No. 45) 1889	—

NWP STANDARD GAUGE LOCOMOTIVES

4-4-0 (AMERICAN) TYPE

Number	Former Numbers	Year	Builder	Class	Cylinders	Drivers	Disposition
1[1]	FB&SE 1st 1				12x18	41	
2nd 1[2]	1st NWP 3, SF&NW 2, ER&E 2 "Eureka"	1884	Baldwin (7400)	Un	13x22	49	R 12-4-1916
2	SF&NW 1, ER&E 1	1883	Baldwin (7013)	Un	13x22	50	R 7-15-1920
2nd 3[3]	O&E 6, E&KR6	1887	Baldwin (8947)	Un	14x24	57	R 8-1-1923
4	SF&NP 1, SF&SJ 2 "San Jose"	1862	R. Norris (1009)	Un	13x22	57	R 7-15-1920
5	SF&NP 5 "Santa Rosa"	1873	Booth (17)	Un	14x22	63	S 6-30-1911
6	SF&NP 2 "J. G. Downey"	1870	Booth (14)	Un	14x22	64	S 7-31-1915
2nd 7	SF&NP 3 "W. J. Ralston"	1870	Booth (15)	Un	14x24	64	R 4-17-1920
8	SF&NP 8 "San Rafael"	1881	Baldwin (5485)	Un	15x24	63	R 5-1-1925
9	SF&NP 9 "Marin"	1883	Grant (1664)	E-43	16x24	59	SB 5-15-1938
10	SF&NP 10 "Healdsburg"	1883	Grant (1665)	E-44	16x24	59	S 6-10-1937
11	SF&NP 6 "Cloverdale"	1878	Grant	Un	16x24	63	S 5-15-1912
12	SF&NP 7 "Petaluma"	1878	Grant	Un	16x24	63	R 11-11-1926
13	SF&NW 6, AT&SF 07, 45, 25 "Colorado Springs"	1875	Baldwin (3831)	Un	16x24	57	R 4-8-1929
14	SF&NP 14 "Tiburon"	1888	Grant	E-45	16x24	62	S 9-26-1936
15	1st NWP 7, SF&NW 7, AT&SF 049, 103, NM&SP 503-203 "C. C. Jackson"	1878	Baldwin (4416)	Un	17x24	61	R 10-21-1930
16	SF&NW 4, ER&E 4	1880	Penn RR (1031)	Un	17x24	59	R 10-21-1930
17	SF&NP 17 "Lytton"	1889	Rogers (4155)	E-46	17x24	63	S 9-21-1935
18	SF&NP 16 "Vichy"	1889	Rogers (4154)	Un	18x24	63	S 8-8-1910[4]
19	SF&NP 12 "Peter Donahue"	1884	Rogers (3305)	E-47	18x24	61	S 7-13-1937
20	SF&NP 13 "Tom Rogers"	1884	Rogers (3306)	E-47	18x24	61	S 9-26-1936
21	SF&NP 24	1904	Baldwin (24035)	E-48	18x24	69	S 6-10-1937
22		1908	American (44959)	E-49	18x24	69	S 10-1-1938
23		1908	American (44960)	E-49	18x24	69	S 3-14-1949
51		1914	American (54580)	E-50	19x26	63	S 2-28-1938
52		1914	American (54581)	E-50	19x26	63	S 2-28-1938
53		1914	American (54582)	E-50	19x26	63	S 5-6-1938
54		1914	American (54583)	E-50	19x26	63	S 4-30-1938

0-4-0 TANK TYPE

Number	Former Numbers	Year	Builder	Class	Cylinders	Drivers	Disposition
99	SF&NP 99	1887	E. Jardine	Un	6x12		Sold, 2-18-1910[5]

No.	Owner	4-6-0 (TEN-WHEELER)		TYPE			Disposition
101	SF&NP 18 "Skaggs"	Rogers (4212)	1889	Un	16x24	57	R 9-30-1928
102	SF&NP 15 "Eureka"	Grant	1888	Un	18x24	55	R 5-31-1929
103	SF&NP 20	Richmond (3304)	1901	T-43	18x24	57	S 12-15-1935
104	CNW 31	Richmond (3303)	1901	T-43	18x24	57	S 9-26-1936
105	SF&NP 21	American (25620)	1902	T-44	19x26	57	S 7-17-1934
106	SF&NP 25, CNW 32	American (25621)	1902	T-44	19x26	57	S 3-10-1934
107	SF&NP 22	Baldwin (23933)	1904	T-44	19x26	57	S 4-10-1937
108	SF&NP 23	Baldwin (23951)	1904	T-44	19x26	57	S 10-21-1948
109	CNW 30,1	Baldwin (18179)	1900	T-45	19x26	57	S 10-14-1948
110	SF&NP 19	Baldwin (17759)	1900	T-45	19x26	57	S 4-10-1937
111		American (44955)	1908	T-46	19x26	57	S 10-31-1949
112		American (44956)	1908	T-46	19x26	57	Held for R&LHS Museum
113		American (44957)	1908	T-46	19x26	57	S 10-3-1947
114		American (44958)	1908	T-46	19x26	57	S 2-6-1947
130		American (49089)	1910	T-47	20x28	63	S 7-18-1938
131		American (49090)	1910	T-47	20x28	63	S 7-18-1938
132		American (49091)	1910	T-47	20x28	63	S 10-1-1938
133		American (49092)	1910	T-47	20x28	63	S 10-31-1938
134		American (51536)	1912	T-48	20x28	63	S 12-31-1940
135		American (51537)	1912	T-48	20x28	63	S 11-30-1940
136		American (54578)	1914	T-49	20x28	63	S 10-31-1940
137		American (54579)	1914	T-49	20x28	63	S 12-31-1940
138		American (54975)	1914	T-49	20x28	63	S 12-31-1940
139		American (54976)	1914	T-50	20x28	63	S 3-27-1947
140		American (54977)	1914	T-50	20x28	63	SB 8-15-1954ª
141		American (54978)	1914	T-50	20x28	63	S 3-31-1954
142		Baldwin (55356)	1922	T-51	20x28	63	S 8-7-1953
143		Baldwin (55473)	1922	T-51	20x28	63	S 12-28-1953
170	LV&T 4	Baldwin (30105)	1907	T-52	21x26	57	S 12-21-1950
171	LV&T 5	Baldwin (30106)	1907	T-52	21x26	57	S 12-14-1946
172	LV&T 8	Baldwin (31094)	1907	T-52	21x26	57	S 11-18-1948
178	BF&GF 11	Baldwin (29726)	1906	T-53	21x28	63	S 1-21-1954
179	NWP 129, LV&T 12	American (44753)	1907	T-54	21x28	63	S 8-4-1952
180	NWP 160	American (44979)	1914	T-55	21x28	57	S 9-21-1952
181	NWP 161	American (54980)	1914	T-55	21x28	57	DCMP 7-1-1955
182		Baldwin (55351)	1922	T-59	21x28	57	D-L-LA 11-21-1955
183		Baldwin (55470)	1922	T-59	21x28	57	DCMP 5-6-1955
184		Baldwin (55471)	1922	T-59	21x28	57	S 11-23-1953

Number	Former Numbers	Year	Builder	Class	Cylinders	Drivers	Disposition
2-6-2 TANK TYPE							
201	CNW 33	1903	Baldwin (22446)	Un	17x22	47	R 10-21-1930
202	CNW 34	1903	Baldwin (22474)	PR-3	17x22	47	Sold, 10-31-1937
2-4-2 TANK TYPE							
225	FB&SE 2nd 1	1888	Porter	CO-1	12x18	41	Sold, 10-31-1937
0-6-0 SWITCHER TYPE							
226	FB&SE 2, AT&SF 2232, 122	1880	Hinkley	Un	16x24	50	S 1910
227		1910	American (48037)	S-20	19x24	50	S 11-5-1948
228		1910	American (48038)	S-20	19x24	50	S 1-27-1949
229		1914	American (54981)	S-21	19x24	50	S 10-14-1948
230		1914	American (54982)	S-21	19x24	50	S 11-30-1948
231		1914	American (54983)	S-21	19x24	50	S 6-21-1950
SHAY							
251	NWR 1, CNW 32	1904	Lima (909)	SH-1	13½x15	40	Sold, 1-1-35[7]
HEISLER							
255[8]	HL 7, JRL 7	1912	Heisler (1254)	Un	16½x14	40	Sold, 2-27-1924[9]
2-6-0 (MOGUL) TYPE							
300	SP 1714, 2140	1901	Cooke (2624)	M-4	20x28	63	S 11-18-1936
301	SP 1716, 2142	1901	Cooke (2626)	M-4	20x28	63	S 11-18-1936
351	NWP 151, SF&NW 3, ER&E 3 "Defender"	1887	Baldwin (8776)	Un	13x22	39	S 9-20-1916
352	NWP 152, SF&NW 5, ER&E 5, AT&SF 0179, GS&SF 314, 65	1886	Baldwin (8092)	Un	17x24	55	R 5-31-1929
353	NWP 153	1908	American (45284)	M-22	18x24	57	S 12-15-1935
354	NWP 154	1908	American (45285)	M-22	18x24	57	S 9-12-1935

[1] Number reserved for this engine, but never applied.
[2] Renumbered 1911.
[3] Acquired 1911.
[4] Destroyed in wreck near Ignacio.
[5] North Bend Lumber Co.
[6] At Tiburon, Calif.
[7] To Mason, Walsh, Atkinson & Kerr.
[8] Acquired 1-21-1922.
[9] Shaw-Bertram Lumber Co., Klamath Falls, Ore.

NWP NARROW GAUGE LOCOMOTIVES

Number	Former Numbers	Year	Builder	Wheel Arrangement	Cylinders	Drivers	Disposition
80	NWP 7, NS 7 "Tamalpais"	1875	Baldwin (3721)	4-4-0	12x16	42	S 5-1-1908
81	NWP 4, NS 4 "Olema"	1874	Baldwin (3629)	4-4-0	12x16	42	S 5-1-1908
82	NWP 11, NS 11 "Marin"	1876	Baldwin (3842)	4-4-0	12x16	42	S 6-30-1911
83	NWP 3, NS 3, NPC 3 "Tomales"	1875	Baldwin (3722)	4-4-0	12x16	42	S 5-1913
84	NWP 20, NS 20, NPC 20	1900	NPC (1)	4-4-0	13x18	47	R 7-15-1920
86	NWP 19, SPC 15	1884	Baldwin (7236)	4-4-0	14x18	52	Acq. from SPC 7-28-1907, sold DML&I 6-24-20, S '26
87	NWP 10, SPC 10	1880	Baldwin (4960)	4-4-0	14x18	49	Acq. from SPC 12-9-1907, S 11-19-1917
88	NWP 8, NS 8, NPC 8, "Bully Boy"	1877	Mason (584)	0-6-6	12x18	37	S 1911
89	NWP 2, NS 2, NPC 2 "San Rafael"	1874	Mason (537)	0-4-4	12x16	42	S 1911
90	NWP 16, NS 15, NPC 15	1886	Brooks (1886)	4-4-0	15x20	48	S 12-15-1935
91	NWP 16, NS 16, NPC 16	1894	Brooks (2421)	4-4-0	15x20	48	Sold, S 10-17-1934
92	NWP 14, NS 14, NPC 14	1891	Brooks (1885)	4-4-0	16x20	48	Sold, S 10-17-1934
93	NWP 85, 17, SPC 14	1884	Baldwin (7249)	4-4-0	14x18	52	Acq. from SPC 7-14-1907, sold, S 10-17-1934
94	NWP 144, 21, SPC 20	1887	Baldwin (8486)	4-6-0	16x20	50	Acq. from SPC 1-2-1908, S 10-17-1934
95	NWP 145, 18, NS 18, NPC 18	1899	Brooks (3418)	4-6-0	16x22	55	S 12-15-1935
195	NWP 13, NS 13, NPC 13	1883	Baldwin (6611)	2-6-0	14x18	39	S 12-15-1935
321	NWP 40, NS 40, D&RG 44, "Texas Creek"	1880	Baldwin (4974)	2-8-0	15x18	36	Purch. 1903 from D&RG, S 12-31-1910
322	NWP 33, NS 33, DSS&A 33, H&C 2, "Tamarack"	1885	Baldwin (7677)	2-8-0	16x20	37	Purch. 1903 from DSS&A, R 9-30-1911
323	NWP 31, NS 31, DSS&A 31, H&C 3, "Oscelo"	1885	Baldwin (7676)	2-8-0	16x20	37	Purch. 1903 from DSS&A, S 7-31-1915

The NWP purchased 3 narrow gauge steam dummies by the contractor building the Baltimore Park-Greenbrae cut-off in 1908. Bearing NWP numbers 23, 24 and 25, they were used on the SQ&SR Line for a short time and scrapped.

ABBREVIATIONS

A&SE—Albion & Southeastern
AT&SF—Atchison, Topeka & Santa Fe
BF&GF—Bullfrog & Goldfield
CNW—California Northwestern
CP—Central Pacific
D&RG—Denver & Rio Grande (ng)
DCMP—Delivered Calif. Metals, Pittsburg Scrap
D-L-LA—Delivered Luria Bros., Los Angeles Scrap
D-L—Dollar Lumber Co. (ng)
DML&L—Duncan Mills Land & Lumber Co. (ng)
DSS&A—Duluth, South Shore & Atlantic (ng)
F&KR—Eureka & Klamath River
FR&F—Eel River & Eureka
FB&SE—Fort Bragg & Southeastern

GC&SF—Gulf Coast & Santa Fe
H&C—Hancock & Calumet (ng)
HB&T—Humboldt Bay & Trinidad
HRI—Horseshoe Lumber Co.
JRL—Jordan River Lumber Co.
L—Leased
LV&T—Las Vegas & Tonopah
ng—narrow gauge
NM&SP—New Mexico & Southern Pacific
NPC—North Pacific Coast (ng)
NS—North Shore (ng)
NWP—Northwestern Pacific
NWR—Northwestern Redwood Co.

O&E—Oregon & Eureka
R—retired
R&LHS—Railway & Locomotive Historical Society
S—scrapped
SB—stationary boiler
SF&SJ—San Francisco & San Jose
SF&NP—San Francisco & Northern Pacific
SF&NW—San Francisco & Northwestern
SQ&SR—San Quentin & San Rafael (ng)
SP—Southern Pacific
SPC—South Pacific Coast (ng)
Un—unclassified

EXCERPTS FROM THE SECOND ANNUAL REPORT OF THE SAN FRANCISCO AND NORTH PACIFIC RAILWAY CO., JUNE 30th, 1891.

The following pages contain selected sections from the annual report of a small railroad operating in the nineties. The flavor of the times and the comparative simplicity of operations are amazing to one used to the complexities of today. Imagine any railroad settling a claim for a broken leg "without payment of any money"; forcing a County to accept for taxes what the railroad "deemed legal and correct"; or making a station agent pay out of his own pocket the freight claim he did not collect. The zeal of the accountant in having every pound of rail, every tie, culvert, flat wheel and unvarnished caboose carefully listed in his report is refreshing.

The back end sheets contain a performance chart from this same report of engines and steamers. It is an interesting sidelight to note that it took $14,480 in engineers' wages to keep 18 engines on the road for a whole year.

San Francisco and North Pacific Railway Company.

SAN FRANCISCO, CAL., July 15th, 1891.

REPORT OF THE PRESIDENT AND DIRECTORS.

To the Stockholders of the San Francisco and North Pacific Railway Company:

The Board of Directors herewith submit their Second Annual Report, with the accompanying data, showing the physical and financial condition of your property, at the close of the fiscal year ending June 30, 1891.

	MILES OF MAIN AND BRANCH LINES.	MILES OF SIDE TRACKS.	TOTAL LENGTH OF ALL TRACKS.
Tiburon to Ukiah, Main Line	106.00	18.72	124.72
Donahue to Junction with Main Line	5.76	.39	6.15
Fulton to Guerneville	17.61	3.42	21.03
Santa Rosa to Sebastopol	6.25	.15	6.40
Ignacio to Glen Ellen	26.63	1.85	28.48
Total	162.25	24.53	186.78

The length of side tracks has been increased 1.05 miles during the year.

Of the 162.25 miles, 106.20 are laid with 56 lb. steel rails, and the remainder with 50 and 56 lb. iron rails.

There has not been any change in the trestles, which remain at the aggregate length of 36,989$\frac{9}{16}$ feet.

Of the bridging:

> 279 2-10 feet are iron bridges.
> 585 feet are combination.
> 984 feet are wooden.

The wooden Howe Truss Span of 181 feet 4 inches in length over the Russian river, on the Guerneville branch, was so generally worn out that a new bridge had to be constructed. In view of the heavy traffic on this branch, it was considered necessary to build a stronger bridge, and accordingly the wooden structure was replaced by a Pratt combination (steel and wood) truss of 184 feet 10½ inches in length, at a total cost of $6,735.30. Although this work was of a betterment nature, the entire expenditure was charged to working expenses.

There are nine tunnels on the line, their aggregate length being 8,985 feet. Of these tunnels six are timbered throughout, the remainder being partly timbered; portions of them having been built through solid basalt rock.

During the year 135^{916} tons of new 56 lb. steel rails have been put in the track, at a total cost of _____ $5,935.60

Less 134^{356} tons of iron rails taken out of track, the value of which amounted to _____ $4,233.55

Leaving the net cost _____ $1,702.05 which has been charged to capital account.

There has also been expended and charged to capital account during the year, the following:

For new rolling stock	$ 1,676.04
For new sidings	485.75
For new buildings	19,510.27
For miscellaneous	87,606.60
For Ukiah extension	583.68
For Guerneville extension	5,461.50
For Sebastopol extension	3,311.61
Total	$118,608.45

The following table shows the general income account of your company for the fiscal year ending June 30th, 1891, in comparison with the previous year.

The Gross Earnings for the Year were:

	YEAR ENDING JUNE 30, 1891.		YEAR ENDING JUNE 30, 1890.	
	PER CENT	AMOUNT	AMOUNT	PER CENT
From passengers	50.02	$416,479.01	$380,454.86	50.37
" freight	43.57	362,834.57	329,070.57	43.57
" mail service	2.54	21,136.15	12,382.24	1.64
" express service	1.93	16,056.69	14,920.55	1.98
" miscellaneous sources	1.94	16,141.12	18,465.46	2.44
Totals	100.00	$832,647.54	$755,293.68	100.00

The Operating Expenses were:

For conducting transportation	20.72	$172,495.80	$153,497.32	20.32
" motive power	13.07	108,811.96	114,699.62	15.19
" maintenance of cars	2.22	18,526.51	19,588.41	2.59
" maintenance of way	17.09	142,281.02	138,937.00	18.39
" general expenses	9.10	75,737.13	75,060.93	9.94
Totals	62.20	$517,852.42	$501,783.28	66.43
Net earnings for the year	37.80	$314,795.12	$253,510.40	33.57

Fixed and other Payments Chargeable against Revenue:

For taxes	3.19	$ 26,610.31	$ 24,000.00	3.18
" interest on first mortgage bonds	24.82	206,633.33	202,778.90	26.85
" sinking funds	3.00	25,000.00	25,000.00	3.31
Totals	31.01	$258,243.64	$251,778.90	33.34
Surplus revenue	6.79	$ 56,551.48	$ 1,731.50	00.23

From the above table it will be seen that the surplus revenue for the year ending June 30th, 1891, was $56,551.48, as against $1,731.50 for the preceding year.

The Company has, therefore, earned a dividend of nearly one per cent on the capital stock during the past year, but, by reason of the surplus having been used for construction purposes, the finances will not admit of any dividend being paid at present.

In comparison with the preceding year, the gross earnings show an increase of $77,353.86, or 10.24 per cent.

Your company has leased a new pleasure resort, naming it "El Campo," situated on the east shore of Marin County, three and one-half miles from Tiburon. A wharf, pavilion and other buildings are being erected, and it is intended to open this resort by the middle of July.

It is confidently expected that this resort will add largely to the revenue of your company, as its close proximity to San Francisco, and being the only pleasure grounds reached by steamers on this Coast, cannot fail to insure good patronage and become a most popular place for a day in the country. It is proposed to use it for picnics, excursions and family outings. By reason of this resort your company will be enabled to make greater use of their steamers, thereby relieving, in a measure, the strain upon the carrying capacity of your railway, now employed to the fullest limits by the constantly growing excursion traffic.

The new double-ender combination (freight and passenger) steamer "Ukiah," was placed in service in January, 1891, and has proved a complete success, both as to stability and speed. This steamer developed the unusual speed of eighteen knots per hour, and is, undoubtedly, the fastest double-ender ferry boat in the world. She has proved her value to your company on many excursions as a passenger steamer, where it was necessary to carry a large number of passengers, and has given great satisfaction to your company and the public in general. This steamer will supply the wants of shippers along your line of road in transferring the products of the counties traversed, so that cars can be landed in San Francisco without breaking bulk, which heretofore were unloaded at Tiburon, and freight conveyed by steamer or schooner to San Francisco. The old manner of handling freight has been very detrimental to many products shipped from and to points on your road, as well as expensive to your company, by reason of the extra labor in loading and unloading.

During the year of 1889-1890, 2.12 miles of track below Guerneville, known as the Guerne-Murphy Railroad, was purchased and improved at a cost of $36,336.42. According to contract with the Sonoma Lumber Company, an additional extension of 1½ miles of track is now being constructed further into the redwood timber, and the estimated cost of such extension is $15,000. When this work is completed, it is expected that lumber and cord wood shipments will be large, and that this extension will be a source of increased freight revenue to your company.

The wood and charcoal business has fallen off somewhat during the past year, on account of the price of coal resuming its normal rate, as against the abnormal and high price of last year.

In lumber, tanbark, brick, flour, wine and fruit, very satisfactory increases have been obtained. The prospects for a heavy fruit business this year have never been more favorable, and by having connection with the Southern Pacific Company, whereby all classes of freight can be shipped direct from producers to Eastern points, it can conservatively be expected that the freight traffic results will be eminently satisfactory.

In Basalt rock shipments, a decrease of 18,940 tons with a corresponding decrease of $12,485.56 in revenue has occurred. In the previous year this class of freight was 17.44 per cent of the total tonnage, whereas this year it has fallen to 7.72 per cent. The causes for the decline can be briefly stated as follows:

The Board of Supervisors under the last administration, passed an ordinance requiring that six inches of concrete should be put as a foundation under both the Basalt blocks and the Bituminous rock. This ordinance made the work of laying the Basalt blocks so expensive, and was so manifestly in favor of the Bituminous rock, that the Basalt block men immediately ceased shipping. The apathy in the Basalt block market continued until the new administration, when the new Board of Supervisors, after having the matter under consideration for many weeks, passed the following ordinances, which were duly ratified by the mayor:

"For the Basalt block pavement, it is provided that the roadbed shall first be excavated to a depth of fourteen inches, and the blocks set thin edge up, on a six inch layer of sand."

"For the Bituminous rock pavement, it is provided that the roadbed shall be excavated to a depth of eight and one-half inches, a six inch layer of concrete being first laid down after the most approved plan, and upon this laid a coating of Bituminous rock two and one-half inches thick."

This action was considered a signal victory for the Basalt blocks. So quickly has the effects of the new ordinance been felt, that already the Basalt block shipments are assuming the usual proportion of your freight traffic, and undoubtedly this business will be greatly enhanced by the present favorable ordinances.

The roadway, structures and equipment are in excellent condition generally, and no efforts have been spared to keep your property up to the standard.

For the satisfactory results obtained and for the efficient services rendered by your officers in the several departments, and all persons employed under their direction, the acknowledgment of the stockholders and directors are due.

Respectfully submitted,

J. F. BURGIN,
President.

San Francisco and North Pacific Railway Company.
OFFICE OF GENERAL MANAGER.

———

SAN FRANCISCO, July 20th, 1891.

To the President and Board of Directors of the San Francisco and North Pacific Railway Company.

GENTLEMEN:—I herewith respectfully submit the Second Annual Report of the Operating Department of the San Francisco and North Pacific Railway, for the year ending June 30th, 1891.

The total train mileage for the year was 389,430 miles, and the total steamer mileage was 38,547 miles.

TRACK AND ROADWAY.

Tons of steel rail laid to replace iron rails.. 135 916 lbs.
Tons of second class iron to replace worn out rails...................... 164
New ties replaced in the main track..38,830
New ties replaced in sidings 2,800
Miles of fence constructed.. 2
Carloads of ballast distributed on main line................................. 1,200
Carloads of ballast distributed on the Sonoma Valley branch...... 650
Carloads of ballast distributed on the Sebastopol branch............ 40
Carloads of ballast for releveling station grounds........................ 110

San Rafael,	Schellville,
Ignacio,	Buena Vista,
Healdsburg,	Madrone,
Harvey's Ranch, Hopland,	Chauvets,
Rose's Ranch,	Glen Ellen,

Aggregating 5,546 feet.

New right of way has been obtained, and one-half mile of roadbed near Cloverdale has been removed to it on account of the change in the course of the Russian river.

A temporary connection has been made from the Sonoma Valley branch to the Southern Pacific System, for the interchange of traffic between your road and Eastern points, and an arrangement entered into between the two companies, which should result in increased prosperity to the country traversed by your lines, and a corresponding increase in the traffic of the road.

BRIDGES.

A new combinaiton bridge, 181 feet 4 inch span, over the Russian river, on the Fulton and Guerneville branch, has been constructed, to replace the wooden Howe Truss bridge, and new pile trestle approaches of 60 and 120 feet respectively, constructed.

Trestles and bridges on the main line, between Tiburon and Cloverdale have been rebuilt.

All the piles, caps, stringers and ties, showing weakness or decay, have been replaced.

The Santa Rosa bridge has been repaired, on account of derailment of a locomotive thereon.

Trestles and bridges on the Sonoma Valley branch have been strengthened to carry the heavier traffic of our standard gauge.

200 piles were driven on the Fulton and Guerneville branch; 75 new piles driven on the Tiburon wharf, and extensive repairs made on the ferry slip.

All the bridges, trestles, cattle guards, fences, etc., have been maintained, and the physical condition of all wooden structures has been much improved since my last report.

BUILDINGS.

New station houses have been built at:

Largo,	Sebastopol,
Preston,	Schuetzen Park.
Caliente,	

New coal and sand houses have been built at Tiburon, and watchmen's houses at Brickyard and Novato Drawbridges.

Station buildings at Glen Ellen, Vineyard and Schellville, have been raised to conform to the change of gauge.

The Sonoma Hotel at Tiburon has been raised and placed on a new foundation.

Nine station houses have been re-painted.

Freight and passenger platforms have been constructed, wherever required, and general repairs of buildings maintained.

LOCOMOTIVES.

Three Engines have been thoroughly repaired.	Four Engines painted and varnished.
Four Engines have had ordinary repairs.	Three Engines varnished.

The heavy repairs consist of:

Four New Steel Tires to replace old.	Two New Cross Heads.
One New Driving Wheel.	One New Flue Sheet.
One New Tender Truck.	Sixty-four New Wheels.
Two re-built Tender Trucks.	Six New Axles.
Two New Smoke Stacks.	One New Engine Truck.
Five New Pilots.	Two sets of Flues, re-set.
One New Cab.	Twelve Engine Tires, turned.
Two New Piston Rods.	

PASSENGER CARS.

Nine Passenger Cars, thoroughly repaired, repainted and varnished.
Fifteen Passenger Cars, ordinary repairs, repainted and varnished.
Three Passenger Cars, ordinary repairs and varnished.
Fifty-two New Wheels.

FREIGHT CARS.

Twenty-five Box-cars received repairs exceeding..................................$25.00
Forty-four Flat-cars received repairs exceeding.................................... 25.00
Nine Hand-cars received repairs exceeding... 25.00
Five Push-cars received repairs exceeding.. 25.00

Six Box-cars, repainted.   One Caboose Car repainted.
Ten Flat-cars, repainted.   Twenty New Wheels.

CONSTRUCTED.

Three Push-cars.   Eight Baggage Trucks (large).
One Section Dump-car.

One Box-car and one Flat-car have been wrecked; one Flat-car has been
    burned; and four Flat-cars taken out of service.
Marine Pile Driver, new tubes, tube sheets and engine thoroughly repaired.
Land Pile Driver, Engine and Coal Hoisting Engine thoroughly repaired.

STEAMERS.

The new double and ferry transfer steamer "Ukiah," of 2564.42 gross tonnage, was put in service January 8th, 1891, and her performance since that date has been most satisfactory.

The steamer "Tiburon" has been furnished with one new shaft, to replace a broken one, and her engine, boilers and wood work thoroughly repaired, and the steamer repainted.

The steamer "James M. Donahue," has had light repairs during the year, and all the steamers are, at present, in good serviceable condition.

CONSTRUCTION.

The following improvements now under way, and soon to be completed, are:

Extension of the Guerneville branch, 1½ miles into the redwood forests,
    west of Guerneville.

Construction of a wharf and slip at Tiburon, with the necessary tracks for
    transferring loaded freight cars on to the steamer "Ukiah," to be
    transported across the bay, and landed on the Union Belt Railroad,
    now being constructed by the State, thus saving the cost, delay and
    breakage in transferring freight from cars to steamer, and from steamer
    to wharf.

Construction of a new wharf and pavilion at the new picnic grounds "El
    Campo," to be used for picnics and excursion parties.

ACCIDENTS.

No passengers have been killed or injured while traveling on the trains or boats of your company, during the year; two women were slightly injured by jumping from the train before it came to a full stop.

One conductor was knocked from a train by coming in contact with the side of a bridge, and slightly injured.

Two brakemen received slight injuries to their hands while coupling cars.

One section man had his leg broken while dumping a car of ballast.

One tramp was struck and killed by a locomotive, while asleep on the track, and another while crossing the track had his legs broken by being struck by the pilot of the locomotive.

Two freight train accidents have occurred at Brickyard draw-bridge, both caused by the bridge being unlawfully opened by schooner men who wished to pass their schooners through. In the first instance, two cars were run into the creek, slightly damaged, and $300 worth of freight destroyed; and in the other, four cars went into the creek, two of them being badly damaged, and $600 worth of freight destroyed.

A passenger train was derailed near Santa Rosa by the switch being misplaced, the engine and two cars leaving the track, the former running on to the Santa Rosa Creek bridge, and was partially turned over. The damage to locomotive, bridge and cars amounted to about $1,000. No person was injured.

No other accidents to persons or property worth mentioning, have occurred during the year.

Acknowledgments are due to the various officers and employees in all departments, for the satisfactory operations of the road during the past year.

Very respectfully,

H. C. WHITING,
General Manager.

San Francisco and North Pacific Railway Co.
OFFICE OF GENERAL COUNSEL.

———

SAN FRANCISCO, CAL., July 1st, 1891.

J. F. BURGIN, ESQ.,
    President S. F. & N. P. R'y Co.

DEAR SIR:—I beg to submit the following report of litigations of the San Francisco and North Pacific Railway Company submitted to my care during the year ending June 30th, 1891.

S. F. & N. P. RY. CO. *vs.* BOARD OF SUPERVISORS, MARIN COUNTY.

Proceedings brought and writ of certiorari obtained in the Superior Court of Marin County, enjoining the collecting of taxes for the fiscal year 1890-91. Compromised by the Board of Supervisors of that county passing a resolution accepting the amount of money offered by the Company as being the just and legal amount.

S. F. & N. P. RY. *vs.* BOARD OF SUPERVISORS OF SONOMA COUNTY,
AND STATE BOARD OF EQUALIZATION.

Proceedings brought in the Superior Court, Sonoma County, and writ of certiorari obtained restraining the collection of taxes for the fiscal year 1890-91. Matter compromised by Board of Supervisors passing a resolution to accept the amount offered by the Company, which the Company deemed legal and correct.

S. F. & N. P. RY. CO. *vs.* BOARD OF SUPERVISORS OF MENDOCINO
COUNTY AND STATE BOARD OF EQUALIZATION.

Proceedings brought in Superior Court, Mendocino County, and writ of certiorari obtained, enjoining the collection of taxes for the fiscal year 1889-90. Litigation settled by the Board of Supervisors resolving to accept the amount offered by the company as being the just and legal amount.

About $3,000 was saved to the company by these suits.

PAFF *vs.* S. F. & N. P. RY. CO.
Justices' Court, San Francisco.

Action brought to recover $299.00 for loss of baggage by a passenger. Verdict rendered in favor of plaintiff for $70.00 and costs. The action is now on appeal and an attempt is being made to settle it without further trial. The defense is that the articles lost did not come within the meaning of the term baggage.

CLAIM OF S. F. & N. P. RY. CO. *vs*. E. S. SALOMON AND
THE G. A. R. POST, NO. 8

This is a claim for $82.60 for transportation on excursion to Glen Ellen; not yet settled.

PIERCE POWERS *vs*. S. F. & N. P. RY. CO.
Marin County.

Claim for damages by the colliding of the engine with Pierce Powers' team, which he was driving at the time. This matter was contested out of court and finally settled for a small amount.

HENDRICKS *vs*. S. F. & N. P. RY. CO.

Suit for killing a horse; settled by payment of reduced sum, to-wit: $50.00.

STEVE BARSETHY *vs*. S. F. & N. P. RY. CO.

Claim for damages for breaking his leg; matter adjusted without payment of any money.

YANDLE & GLYNN—INSOLVENCY.

This firm was allowed by Agent at Santa Rosa to take cargo of lumber without paying freight. As Agent had given bond agreeing not to let freight go without payment, I had freight claim assigned to him and brought suit in his name against Yandle & Glynn, who then went into insolvency, and he is and has been engaged in collecting dividends from the assignee. In the meantime the Company has obtained the whole amount from Agent.

Respectfully submitted,

CHARLES F. HANLON,
General Counsel.

References

BOOKS

BANCROFT, HUBERT HOWE, *History of California,* Vol. VII, The History Company, San Francisco, 1892

CARPENTIER, AURELIUS O. and PERCY H. MILLBERRY, *History of Mendocino and Lake Counties, California, with biographical sketches,* Historic Record Company, Los Angeles, 1914

COY, OWEN C., *The Humboldt Bay Region, 1850-1875, a study in the American colonization of California,* California State Historical Association, Los Angeles, 1929

DAGGETT, STUART, *Chapters on the History of the Southern Pacific,* Ronald Press, New York, 1922

DANA, JULIAN, *The Man Who Built San Francisco,* The Macmillan Company, New York, 1937

EDDY, J. M., *In the Redwood's Realm, by-ways of wild nature and highways of industry as found under forest shades and amidst clover blossoms in Humboldt County, California,* D. S. Stanley and Company, San Francisco, 1893

GREGORY, TOM, *History of Sonoma County, California, with biographical sketches,* Historic Record Company, Los Angeles, 1911

HAMM, MRS. LILLIE E., *History and Business Directory of Humboldt County, descriptive of the natural resources, delightful climate, picturesque scenery, beautiful homes, the only county in the state containing no chinamen,* Daily Humboldt Standard, Eureka, 1890

HARPENDING, ASBURY, *The Great Diamond Hoax and Other Stirring Incidents in the Life of Asbury Harpending,* The James H. Barry Company, San Francisco, 1913

Humboldt County Souvenir, Times Publishing Company, Eureka, 1904

HUNT, ROCKWELL DENNIS and NELLIE VAN DE GRIFT SANCHEZ, *A Short History of California,* Thomas Y. Crowell, New York, 1929

IRVINE, LEIGH H., *History of Humboldt County, California,* Historic Record Company, Los Angeles, 1915

KNEISS, GILBERT HAROLD, *Bonanza Railroads,* Stanford University Press, Stanford, California, 1941

MACMULLIN, JERRY, *Paddlewheel Days in California,* Stanford University Press, Stanford, California, 1944

MCCUE, DR. J. S., *McCue's Plain Talk,* Corte Madera, California, 1907

MCNAIR, JACK and JERRY MACMULLIN, *Ships of the Redwood Coast,* Stanford University Press, Stanford, California, 1945

MUNRO-FRASER, J. P., *History of Sonoma County,* Alley, Bowen and Company, San Francisco, 1880

MUNRO-FRASER, J. P., *History of Marin County, California,* Alley, Bowen and Company, San Francisco, 1880

PALMER, LYMAN L., *History of Mendocino County,* Alley, Bowen and Company, San Francisco, 1881

PHELPS, ALONZO, *Contemporary Biography of California's Representative Men,* A. L. Bancroft and Company, San Francisco, 1881

POMEROY, C. P., *Reports of Cases Determined in the Supreme Court of the State of California,* Bancroft-Whitney Company, San Francisco, 1906

QUIGLEY, DR. HUGH, *The Irish Race in California and on the Pacific Coast,* A. Roman and Company, San Francisco, 1878

San Rafael Illustrated and Described, showing its advantages for homes. W. W. Elliot and Company, Oakland, 1884

SCHERER, JAMES A. B., *The Lion of the Vigilantes, William T. Coleman, and the Life of Old San Francisco,* Bobbs-Merrill, New York, 1939

SWASY, W. F., *The Early Days and Men of California,* Pacific Press Publishing Company, Oakland, 1891

THOMPSON, ROBERT A., *Historical and Descriptive Sketch of Sonoma County, California,* L. H. Everts and Company, Philadelphia, 1877

WINN, W. B., *Souvenir of Marin County, California,* Marin County Journal, San Rafael, 1893

YOUNG, JOHN P., *San Francisco, a History of the Pacific Coast Metropolis,* S. J. Clarke Publishing Company, Chicago, 1912

MANUSCRIPTS

Colonel Frederick A. Bee's identification with the history of California (Bancroft Library)

General Patrick Edward Connor (Bancroft Library)

Albert S. Dutton (Kneiss collection)

————— Holden (Society of California Pioneers)

Adolph Mailliard, 1819- (Bancroft Library)

REPORTS, ETC.

North Pacific Coast R. R. of Calif. Prospectus, San Francisco, 1873

The North Pacific Coast R. R. Co. of Calif. Prospectus, 1879

Report of the Board of Commissioners of Transportation to the Legislature of the State of California, Sacramento, 1877

San Francisco & Northern Railway Co. Private and confidential prospectus of the San Francisco and Northern Railway Company, accompanied with report of Mr. L. M. Clement, first assistant engineer of the Central Pacific R. R. Co. New York, 1879

Second Annual Report of the San Francisco and North Pacific Railway Co. and statement of accounts for the year ending June 30th, 1891

MAGAZINE AND PERIODICAL ARTICLES

DOBLE, ROBERT MCF., *The Use of Pacific Coast Water Powers in the Electrical Operation of Railroads,* Official Proceedings Pacific Coast Railway Club, Vol. 6, p. 193, 1904-1905

HOUGHTON, RICHARD, *Redwood Empire Route,* Trains, June, 1946, p. 7

KNEISS, GILBERT HAROLD, *Locomotives of the Union Iron Works,* Bulletin No. 68, The Railway & Locomotive Historical Society, Inc. November, 1946, p. 40

SIEVERS, WALT, *Electric Interurban Service of Marin County,* Western Railroader, November, 1939

SILVERTHORN, WILLIS A., *Early Days on the N. W. P.,* Western Railroader, May, 1944

TRUITT, SHIRLEY M., *The Railroads That Make Up the Present Northwestern Pacific R. R.,* Bulletin No. 29, The Railway & Locomotive Historical Society, October, 1932, p. 26

WOLLNER, W. S., *Historic Phases of the Northwestern Pacific Railroad,* Redwood Empire Review, May 1945-August 1946

NEWSPAPERS

Files of:

Eureka Democratic Standard

Eureka Humboldt Standard

Oakland Tribune

Petaluma Argus

Petaluma Journal and Argus

Quincy Plumas National

Quincy Union

San Francisco Alta California

San Francisco Bulletin

San Francisco Call

San Francisco Chronicle

San Francisco Mining and Scientific Press

San Rafael Herald

San Rafael Independent

San Rafael Marin County Journal

San Rafael Marin County Tocsin

    Santa Rosa Democrat

    Santa Rosa Republican

    Santa Rosa Sonoma Democrat

    Sausalito News

    Stockton Independent

    Ukiah Mendocino Beacon

    Ukiah Mendocino Dispatch and Democrat

and Files of:

    Bancroft's California Guide

    Crofutt's Overland Tourist and Pacific Coast Guide

    Pacific Coast Official Railway & Steamship Guide

    Popular Railroad Guide

    Railroad Gazetteer

    Williams' Pacific Tourist Guide

Timetables and pamphlets of the railroads

Index

Agler, James, 133
Albion & Southeastern R.R., 132
Astoria & Columbia River R.R., 132
Atlas locomotive, 1, 3

Babcock, A. H., 120
Bay City (steamer), 103
Beckwourth Pass, 18, 35, 88, 133
Bee, Frederick A., 9, 10, 11, 15, 16, 27
Bowen, Alfred, 126, 127
Bridges, Col. Lyman, 86
"Bully Boy" (locomotive), 126
Burgin, John, 106

California & Nevada R.R., 130
California & Northern R.R., 131
California Midland R.R., 131
California Northwestern Ry., 109, 125,
   126, 127, 128, 129, 130, 131
California Pacific R.R., 27, 28, 29, 33, 34,
   35, 72, 88
California Pacific Eastern Extension Co.,
   35
California Steam Navigation Co., 35
California Western Ry., 135
Carson, William, 92, 94
Cazadero, 112, 118, 119, 121
Central Pacific R.R., 15, 19, 29, 31, 35,
   37, 38, 39, 44, 50, 56, 86, 88
City of Lakeport (steamer), 103
Clear Lake, 103
Cloverdale, 10, 37, 38
"Cloverdale" (locomotive), 62
Cloverdale & Ukiah R.R., 86
"Coffee-Grinder" (locomotive), 108
Cohen, A. A., 82
Coleman, John W., 111
Coleman, William Tell, 32, 33, 43, 45,
   46, 52, 55, 56, 58, 59, 60, 61, 71
Colgate, R. R., 118, 132
Connor, General Patrick, 9, 13, 15, 16, 17,
   32, 91

Contra Costa (steamer), 22, 24, 25, 51, 73
Contra Costa Steam Navigation Co., 1
Corte Madera, 2, 49, 77, 111, 113, 120
Corvallis & Eastern R.R., 132
Cox, Gus, 43
Crew Prismoidal Railway System, 56, 65
Cutter, Joe, 10

de Sabla, Eugene, 118, 120, 131, 132
Doherty, John, 75, 76, 77, 81
Donahue, 32, 33, 55, 82
Donahue, James Mervyn, 81, 85, 86, 87,
   88, 97, 98, 105, 107, 108, 133
Donahue, Peter, 15, 19, 29, 31, 33, 34,
   39, 55, 59, 60, 61, 62, 65, 68, 77, 79,
   81, 85, 88, 98, 105
Duncan's Mills, 74, 136, 137
Dutton, Warren, 42, 44, 45, 48, 49, 50,
   57, 58, 76, 83, 121

Eastland, J. G., 76, 111
Eel River, 15, 88, 92, 93, 134, 137, 138
Eel River & Eureka R.R., 88, 91, 92, 94,
   130, 132, 133
Enterprise (steamer), 62
Eureka, 91, 92, 93, 106, 130, 131, 133,
   135, 136, 137, 138
Eureka & Klamath River R.R., 132, 133

Fogg, George, 67
Fort Bragg & Southeastern R.R., 132
Foster, A. W., 106, 107, 108, 109, 125,
   126, 127, 129, 131, 132, 133
Frisbie, General John, 8, 11, 34
Fulton & Guerneville R.R., 68

"General Vallejo" (locomotive), 68
Geyserville, 38
Grant, Ulysses S., 91
Guerneville, 62, 107, 108, 136

Hammond, A. B., 132, 133
Harpending, Asbury, 13, 14, 15, 16, 17, 18, 19, 27, 29, 30, 32, 88, 135, 138
Harriman, E. H., 130, 131, 132
Harris, Robert, 30, 31
Hayes, President Rutherford B., 61, 62
Haystack, 3
Healdsburg, 8, 16, 27, 132
Heydenfeldt, Judge Solomon, 16, 17
Hood, William, 86, 134
Howard, Charles, 41
Humboldt Bay & Eureka R.R., 92

"Jackrabbit" (locomotive), 121
James M. Donahue (steamer), 61, 73, 80

Keddie, Arthur W., 18
Kohn, Joseph, 56, 65, 66, 67, 68
Korbel, Antoine, 62

Latham, Milton Slocum, 27, 29, 34, 35, 37, 49, 57, 59, 71, 72, 74, 75, 76, 82, 88
Levitt, Joe, 4

Mailliard, Adolph, 22, 25, 52
Marin & Napa R.R., 86, 87, 88
Markham, Andrew, 106, 107
Martin, John, 118, 119, 120, 123, 131, 132, 136
McCauley, John F., 9, 13, 15, 16, 17, 18, 19, 23, 27, 29, 32
McCrellish, Fred, 9, 13, 15, 32
McCue, Dr. J. S., 113, 114, 115, 116, 117
McGlynn, Peter, 106
McKenzie, Captain John, 22, 73, 114, 116
McNear, John A., 1, 4
Mill Valley, 111, 112, 119, 120, 121
Mill Valley & Mount Tamalpais Scenic Ry., 112
"Milton S. Latham" (locomotive), 73, 112, 113
Minturn, Charles, 1, 2, 3, 4, 5, 16, 21, 22, 23, 25, 30, 51, 58, 73, 125
Moore, Austin D., 41, 42, 44, 45, 46, 48, 50, 51, 76
Moscow, 74

Napa Valley R.R., 7, 10
Nevada Central R.R., 75
Norfolk, 66, 67
North Pacific Coast R.R., 38, 39, 41, 42, 44, 48, 51, 57, 58, 61, 62, 71, 72, 73, 74, 75, 76, 77, 79, 81, 82, 83, 101, 111, 112, 113, 117, 119

North Pacific Coast Railway Extension Co., 77
North Shore R.R., 119, 121, 122, 130, 131
Northwestern R.R., 111
Northwestern Pacific R.R., 133, 134, 135, 138

"Olema" (locomotive), 48, 49, 121
Oneatta (steamer), 92
Oroville & Virginia City R.R., 18

Pacific Lumber Co., 92, 94, 131
Palmer, Warren S., 134, 135
Payson, Captain A. H., 132, 133
Petaluma, 1, 7, 10, 11, 16, 32, 42, 57, 58, 60, 125, 126
"Petaluma" (locomotive), 62
Petaluma (steamer), 3, 4, 5
Petaluma of Saucelito (steamer), 48, 73
Petaluma & Haystack R.R., 1, 57, 59
Petaluma & Healdsburg R.R., 7
Petaluma & Santa Rosa Ry., 125, 126, 127, 128, 129, 137
"Peter Donahue" (locomotive), 98
Point Reyes, 41, 42, 121, 122, 123, 137
Princess (steamer), 13
Pullman service, 136

Ralston, William C., 15, 17, 19, 34, 39, 65, 135
Ripley, Edward Payson, 130, 131, 132, 133
Romer, John, 16, 18, 19, 32, 135
Rosecrans, General William S., 18
Russian River, 35, 38, 62, 74, 87, 97, 98, 103, 106, 107, 108, 137
Russian River Land & Lumber Co., 41, 76

Sacramento (steamer), 30, 31, 32, 33
San Anselmo, 45, 52, 76, 111, 119
San Francisco & Eureka R.R., 132
San Francisco & Humboldt Bay R.R., 9, 10, 11, 13, 15, 17, 28, 91, 135
San Francisco & Northern Ry., 76
San Francisco & Northern Coast R.R., 27
San Francisco & North Pacific R.R., 17, 28, 29, 31, 33, 34, 35, 39, 55, 59, 60, 62, 68, 79, 81, 85, 87, 99, 102, 105, 106, 108, 109, 131
San Francisco & Northwestern R.R., 132
San Francisco & San Jose R.R., 29, 98
San Francisco & San Rafael R.R., 77
San Francisco, Tamalpais & Bolinas R.R., 111
"San Jose" (locomotive), 31, 32, 33, 59, 62

San Quentin, 21, 52, 53

San Rafael, 13, 21, 39, 41, 42, 43, 45, 47, 49, 59, 60, 71, 74, 77, 80, 119, 121, 137, 138

"San Rafael" (locomotive), 24, 25, 47, 51, 52

San Rafael (steamer), 73, 81, 113, 114, 115, 116, 117

San Rafael & San Quentin R.R., 22, 47, 51, 56, 71, 83, 106, 136

Santa Fe Ry., 130, 132, 133, 134, 135, 137

Santa Rosa, 7, 10, 28, 32, 34, 86, 88, 102, 106, 125, 128, 136

Santa Rosa & Benicia Central R.R., 86

Santa Rosa & Carquinez R.R., 86, 87, 88

Saucelito, 9, 30, 37, 39, 41, 44, 45, 52, 77

"Saucelito" (locomotive), 46, 47, 48

Saucelito (steamer), 73, 74, 82

Saucelito Land & Ferry Co., 44

Sausalito, 112, 118, 120, 122, 123, 136

Sausalito (steamer), 114, 115, 116

Schuyler, Howard, 45, 46, 47

Smith, Sidney V., 22, 106, 107, 108

Sonoma, 8, 65, 68

"Sonoma" (locomotive), 75

Sonoma (steamer), 67, 68

Sonoma & Marin Ry., 56, 57, 58, 59, 60, 61, 62, 68

Sonoma County R.R., 8, 10, 11, 17, 28

Sonoma Valley R.R., 68, 87

Sonoma Valley Extension R.R., 86

Sonoma Valley Prismoidal Ry., 66, 67, 68

Southern Pacific R.R., 39, 86, 87, 88, 94, 106, 113, 130, 132, 133, 135, 136, 137, 138

South Pacific Coast R.R., 121

Stanford, Leland, 37, 39, 86

Stetson, James Burgess, 111, 116, 117

Storey, William, 134

Street, William, 111

Temple, Jackson, 11

Texas & Pacific R.R., 39

"The Redwood" (train), 138

Thomas, William, 112

"Thomas-Stetson" (locomotive), 113

Tiburon, 77, 79, 81, 85, 87, 136

Tiburon (steamer), 80, 114

Tillinghast, W. H., 41, 47

Tomales, 42, 43, 45, 48, 49, 50, 58, 74

"Tomales" (locomotive), 121

Twin Sister (steamer), 29, 30, 31

Ukiah, 86, 88, 97, 98

"Ukiah" (locomotive), 80

Ukiah (steamer), 106

Union Iron Works, 15, 29, 33, 62, 80

Union Pacific R.R., 35

Union Packet Line, 2

Union Wharf & Plank Walk Co., 91

Vallejo, 7, 8, 27, 39

Vallejo & Sonoma County R.R., 8, 11

Valley Road, 130

Vance, John, 91, 92, 94

Walker, James D., 22, 83, 111

Western Pacific R.R., 19, 133

White, Ezekial, 23

White's Hill, 22, 43, 45, 48, 49, 76, 77, 119, 131

Whiting, Henry, 98, 102, 106

Wickersham, I. G., 7, 56, 57, 58, 61

Wilson G. Hunt (steamer), 30

Zook, Frank, 98, 106, 107, 128